BROKEN TO BELIEVE

FINDING LIFE BY COMPLETELY LOSING YOUR HEART TO JESUS

KYLE RILEY

Printed in the United States of America

ISBN: 978-0-9970729-1-4 (paperback edition)

ISBN: 978-0-9970729-0-7 (digital edition)

Foreword by Cornelius Lindsey, Edited by Diane Moore,

Cover designed by Kyle Riley

For information regarding special discounts for bulk orders, please contact us at brokentobelievebook@gmail.com

DEDICATION

To my lovely and beautiful wife, whom God blessed me with, thank you for your loving support and encouragement. You continuously inspire me to be a better husband, father, and man. I love you dearly.

To my child, although you were still in your mother's womb during the production of this book, you were often my motivation during the late nights. You encouraged me during the times I wanted to quit. Daddy loves you.

Most importantly, to the One who has saved me through His undying love and grace, I give Him all of the glory. May His name be lifted up forever. Amen.

Table of Contents

FOREWORD

A broken heart finds rest and restoration in the hands of God. It is by His power that the heart is changed, renewed, and revitalized with new life. He is the skilled Potter, and we are his clay.

Brokenness is essential to the life of the believer. God breaks our prideful heart, and He mends it back together as He wills. There are some men who have never experienced that process. Kyle Riley is not one of those men. The brokenhearted preacher is known by his humility and passion for godly works. The brokenhearted man is submitted to the Lord, and is willing to lay down his life for the cause of the Gospel. Kyle embodies the passion and experience necessary to write a book on this topic.

There are some men who are like friends. They come in your life for a specific purpose. There are other men who are like brothers. The difference is the bond that is created, and this bond is unbreakable. The glue that binds their hearts and pushes them to partner together for godly causes is the Gospel. Kyle is not just a friend. He is a brother.

I am confident that you will find as much comfort in this book as I have. And I only hope and pray that the words you read stir you up to fulfill all God has called you to do. Prepare to be moved. Prepare to be challenged. Prepare to be changed.

Cornelius Lindsey

Author of So, You Want to be Married?, I'm Married. Now, What?, Not For Sale, So, You Want to be a Man?, Learning How to Walk, Suffering in Silence, and Decoding the Silent Man's Language.

www.corneliuslindsey.com

i

INTRODUCTION

"Until our hearts are broken, God's grace cannot enter. Until we recognize that brokenness, the path to new life is obscured."

Rev. Alan M. Gates

Wrecked. Destroyed. Hopeless. These are words that we frequently associate with the thought of someone who is broken. A person who has endured troubling times, pretty much hitting rock bottom, will often identify with this term. Many times, we find ourselves affected by the external happenings of life, placing us in a state of defeat and discouragement. This, without question, is a common emotional and spiritual location for many people – broken. However, there is another form of brokenness that exists. In the literal sense, broken can mean interrupted, disconnected, or separated. These words also serve as descriptions of someone or something that is broken. That something that I am particularly referring to is the heart – the centrality of who you are as a person. This is the form of brokenness that we will address, confront, and analyze. As we lay this foundation, we will build and grow throughout this book.

What does it truly mean to be broken you might ask? Authentic brokenness comes from an internal realization. It is the result of one thing: an encounter with Jesus that shines a beaming light on of your sinfulness. This breaking of the heart consists of an awareness of who you are in relation to a holy and perfect God. It is acknowledgment, which serves as the first step towards repentance. We, as flawed human beings, must realize the seriousness of what separates us from God. That "what" is sin – missing the mark, and falling short of His standard. All of us – Yes ALL of us - are guilty of this, and we will continue to be because we are imperfect. But I've found that a common problem is that many people,

1

Christians included, aren't truly broken over their sin. Their "belief" in God hasn't done such a work in them that produces a sense of disgust and distaste for the wickedness that lies within them. And until this happens, the beautiful assurance of God's grace will be of no true value!

The inspiration for this book comes from a very personal place. It is the result of many of my life experiences that involved denial, curiosity, and even pure rebellion. My own brokenness simply compelled me to encourage and inspire others. Additionally, this book is an expression of my continual growth, repentance, and desire to further know Christ. I prayed fervently during the process of writing this book. It is so important that you do the same while reading it. In saying this, I pray you allow the Holy Spirit to guide you while receiving this information. May your heart and mind be open to not only take in, but intentionally apply in your quest to know God. It must be pragmatic. Our ability to grow in Christ is only inhibited by the rejection of truth. And our delay in spiritual growth is often due to lack of application.

As you navigate through this journey of spiritual renewal, the goal is to allow the Holy Spirit to break you. This is step one, which only comes from personal time with Him. The book itself is only a guide. It isn't the remedy - Prayer is. You will see that I implore you to do a lot of that throughout this time. Prayer is an intimate reach for God's heart, and in turn, allowing Him to reach yours. This is where the next part of the process enters. Once broken, you must then allow the undeserved grace of God to permeate your broken heart, creating an insatiable desire to wholeheartedly follow Jesus; to truly believe. Not believing that Jesus just merely existed, but believing with everything in you that He is who He says He is – the Giver of life. With that belief comes rebirth. To believe in something means to have total confidence in the truth, supporting everything it stands for. Likewise, believing in Jesus entails doing away with living life our way and submitting ourselves to reflect everything Jesus stands for!

It is the anguish of a contrite heart, which leads you to fully believe, experiencing the unconditional love of God. As you read this book, my prayer is that God opens the eyes of your heart, just as mine were opened. No matter where you are spiritually, there is always room for growth. Have you become stagnant in your walk with Christ? Have you come to the point where you know God is calling you to something more? Or are you even just interested in knowing more about Jesus? Whether you're unsure about who God is or you're a devoted believer who has gone to church your whole life, I'm confident you will be enlightened, challenged, and encouraged to undeniably follow Jesus! But it starts with one question: Have you truly been broken?

PRAYER

"God, as I read this, give me a broken heart; one that shows me myself, then produces a desire to experience the glory of Your undeserved grace. As I seek to draw closer to You, give me a hunger to know You intimately. May the Holy Spirit guide me to truth. Lord, make me broken. Broken….to believe."

CHAPTER 1

Who are You really?

"What comes into our minds when we think about God is the most important thing about us."

— A.W. Tozer

I remember that night vividly. "God, I'm sorry!!!" came screaming from the top of my vocal cords. The time had come where I knew something had to change. I was tired; tired of being a liar, saying that I believed in God yet living as if I had no clue who He was. I was tired of playing a role. I was tired being insecure. There is no scarier feeling than being unsure of where you will spend eternity. I remember asking that dreadful question, "If I died tonight, would I go to heaven?" Despite the fact that I had professed Jesus as my Savior and been baptized just a few years prior, my lifestyle in no way reflected that of a person who claimed to know Jesus Christ. And it was because I really didn't know Him. I was tired of *acting* like I had it all together. In reality, I was a young man who was hurting on the inside. There was a gaping hole in my heart with so much emptiness; one that I had attempted to fill time after time with everything under the sun.

As a college student, parties filled my weekends (sometimes week-days) and I sought pleasure in activities and people that ultimately had absolutely nothing to offer but temporary gratification. That night during my senior year, I came to the understanding that my life of sin was a direct result of my failure to truly see God for who He is. Part of me didn't want to see Him properly, because I knew what that would entail – change. I was sitting on the edge of my bed flipping through an old Bible that had been given to me in high school, and was asking God to make Himself

5

known to me. How silly, right? Here I am asking the Creator of the universe to reveal Himself to little ol' me! There are over 7 billion people on this Earth, and I had the nerve to ask Him to consider allowing *me* to see Him? Yes, that's exactly right.

I believe that's what He desires from all of us. He desires an encounter. The truth is I had heard the sermons, read the Bible here and there, and prayed occasionally, but I never had an actual encounter with Jesus; an encounter that forces you to look at your life differently and begin to fine tune certain aspects that aren't pleasing to Him. God was asking me to examine what I was seeking fulfillment in, and where it was taking me. Many of us have found ourselves in this very situation, and if you haven't, I ask you to take a deep look at your life, and assess what it is that you are pursuing to bring you happiness. Is it success? A significant other? A degree or your career? We live in a world that tells us to chase our dreams and accomplish our goals by any means – to live our best life now! This has caused many to measure their worth by status, the accumulation of monetary wealth, and approval from other people who really don't matter. It's honestly the very opposite of what Jesus taught. At the end of the day, those temporal things will not save you. They did not die for you, and they certainly will not be taken with you when you leave here. Essentially, you are struggling to find on earth what will be found only in Christ, and it's a constant chase.

Let's be honest, not everyone has that "Road to Damascus" experience where Jesus blinds you as He did Saul (Acts Ch. 9), immediately changing you. While the Gospel is certainly powerful enough and capable of doing so, change is generally an ongoing process for most of us. It is a journey of growth that takes a constant yielding to the Holy Spirit. No one is perfect, and we will always be faced with temptations to act on our flesh. However, there must come a time in your life where the good news of Jesus Christ enters your heart and starts to do such a work inside of you, that the sin you once loved you now begin to hate; And the God you once rejected and ignored, you now admire and respect!

In this book, I aim to deeply explore what it means to be a follower of Jesus Christ. In doing so, we will examine the surrendering process that so many of us run from, and even fight. We will tackle the issues of the complacent Christian, and prayerfully will yield ourselves to the will of God. This journey begins in a certain place. It is a place that many of us don't want to go, but must venture to. It's a place of honesty, vulnerability, darkness, and discomfort. It is positioning yourself in front of the mirror and being willing to acknowledge what you see. This position is known as being "broken." The starting point to this process is located in the form of one critical question...

WHO IS GOD?

Who is God? What is He like? Naturally, everyone has their personal answers to these questions. However, it's imperative that there is a mutual understanding when answering such questions. That understanding is that the answers themselves SHOULD NOT be personal! When it comes to describing God, the description must derive from what He simply *reveals* about Himself through His Word – The Bible. Failure to do so results in an inaccurate and opinionated view of an infinite God – This coming from finite minds that He Himself created. Why is this so important you might ask? It's important because what we think about God ultimately establishes who we are: how we behave, what we think, and why we think the way we do. It shapes our thoughts and controls our actions. Our view of God is the most essential part of us as people. A.W. Tozer once said, "...the most portentous fact about any man is not what he at a given time may say or do, but what he in his deep heart conceives God to be like."

In essence, I'm not concerned with, nor impressed by, a person's accomplishments and ability to speak well. I don't care how much influence they have. It doesn't matter what his or her title is, or what capabilities they possess. In the grand scheme of things, that all means absolutely nothing. But rather, how do they see God? What do they think of Him? That person's words and actions will then reflect such thoughts. Eternally, that's the only thing that matters.

Often times, our view of God is shaped by the circumstances of life. Personally, I recall how my limited exposure to Christianity as a child created a curious mind that sought to understand Him. Deep down, this hunger for truth burned within me. But because I was never taught, I formed my own opinions about God, which were based on the positive and negative life conditions that arose. This became my truth.

7

THOUGHTS OF A YOUNG MAN

I wasn't raised in church. God was hardly ever discussed in my family's house. The closest thing to spiritual we got was praying over our food prior to eating. Even then, it was a rehearsed prayer that I often sped through just so I could quickly get to eating. My parents separated when I was in 5th grade, and although I saw my father frequently, my mother primarily raised my three younger siblings and me. As a child, I longed to be part of that family that woke up on Sunday mornings, dressed up, piled in the car, and routinely went to church – with my father driving and playing gospel music en route. I desired to be that child running around the church, who knew the Bible stories that are typically taught to kids in Sunday School. I envisioned us going out to lunch as a family after service and talking about what I learned that day. Instead, Sundays in our household usually consisted of us cleaning and doing homework; that's if I wasn't somewhere playing in a basketball tournament.

My only view of church as a child came from occasionally visiting my friend's church during my years in elementary school. His father was a pastor, and whenever I spent the night at his house on Saturdays it was mandatory that we woke up and went to church the next morning. Saturday nights were often restless for me, as I stayed up thinking about what the experience would be like the following morning. I vividly recall feeling out of place every time I attended church. It was small, and I felt like everybody knew I didn't know much about God. For the longest, I felt this sense of not belonging – which ironically many adults feel today about the church…. but we'll get to that later. I believed in God, yet I still felt like everyone at the church had some keen sense that I wasn't saved. One instance during the taking of communion, my friend's father asked me, "Kyle, have you been baptized?" Not having the slightest clue what he was referring to, I shook my head "No." I figured that since I wasn't familiar with the term, I probably hadn't been. And I didn't want to lie and say that I was when I really wasn't.

Subsequently, I watched as my friend took his little cup of grape juice and bread piece from the trays as they were passed around the room. As it was about to be passed down my aisle, his dad whispered to the usher distributing communion, who then passed the tray right over me to the person sitting beside me. "Hold on! Why did I get skipped over?!!" I yelled, in my head. His dad then proceeded to ask the congregation, as is the common procedure, "Has anyone been overlooked?" I threw my hand up in the air so quickly, my arm nearly shot out of its socket. I saw him glance over at me, then carry on with the services. An elderly woman behind me tapped my shoulder and informed me that I could put my hand down. "So I'm not good enough to participate in this ritual?" I thought. I sat and watched everyone place the bread in their mouths, and witnessed their heads tilting back to consume the "blood of Christ." Can you imagine how I felt? Confused would be an understatement! I felt inadequate. And if the church members didn't already know I wasn't saved, they sure enough knew now! There I was, sitting, twiddling my thumbs, blaming my parents for not raising me in church so I could participate in such sacraments.

Feelings of rejection consumed me as a child because no one took time to explain what occurred at that moment, and why. From that point on, my understanding of being a Christian was based on your "ability" to receive communion. I was a kid determined to consume The Lord's supper so I could feel accepted by the church body, instead of actually seeking Him who died for the body. Unfortunately, this whole incident lead to one false idea: my perception of how I thought God viewed me was based on how I thought the church viewed me.

As you can imagine, this experience took a great toll on me. It added to a number of other experiences that ultimately fashioned my incorrect view of God. Our experiences growing up as they relate to God are all different. Some people practically lived in church during their upbringing, some attended occasionally, while others have never stepped foot in a sanctuary a day in their life. Whether completely non-existent or plentiful, your experiences pertaining to God (not just church attendance) have affected you in some way throughout your life. They have shaped your thoughts about Him and why you think them, whether those thoughts be good, bad, or indifferent.

Let's put these experiences to the side for a moment and actually focus on the attributes of God through what He tells us about Himself. As previously stated, this is the only way to truly grasp what we should believe about God. There are many adjectives to describe God. You might have previously heard or used elaborate words like omnipotent, omnipresent, omniscient, even sovereign, but we will focus on three simple yet significant characteristics here:

1. God is **HOLY.**

What does this mean? This means God is set apart. He is consecrated from any other person or being in this universe. He is distinct and separate in nature; perfect in all of His ways. He is pure and righteous. Now, I can list all of these adjectives relating to His holiness, but it means absolutely nothing without a clear comprehension of its relevance. God's holiness is important because, in relation to us, it profoundly depicts the contrast between who He IS, and who we ARE NOT! Frequently, we subconsciously put ourselves in the same category as God – immune, in control, powerful, etc. But we must deliberately remember that He is infinite, existing before time and separate from us. The problem today is that we have reduced God to a mere being; a mythical creature; and even a friend – diminishing his divinity and supremeness in our hearts until His character no longer holds any value. Consequently, a lack of reverence for Him develops that leads to the acceptance of immoral behavior. It is vital that we view Him in light of all of the glory, beauty, and power that He possesses, living with both a fear of and adoration for who He is!

"There is no one holy like the Lord; there is no one besides you; there is no Rock like our God."(1 Samuel 2:2)

"And they were calling to one another: "Holy, holy, holy is the Lord Almighty; the whole earth is full of his glory." (Isaiah 6:3)

2. God is **JUST.**

This is a term we often hear, but don't give much thought to its meaning. By definition, the term "just" can be described as this: agreeing with what is considered morally right or good. As the Creator of the universe, God sets the standard. This means that as the Establisher, he determines what's right and wrong. With that being said, Scripture clearly reveals His hate for sin. And with Him being the One who establishes the rules, He rightly is able to enforce the consequences against those who decide to break them. Many people don't agree with this. Well, when you create your own universe, you can make your own rules. As we previously discussed, God is holy – perfect. Because of this, He hates sin and cannot be in the presence of it. We, being imperfect, are sinners. Therefore, He MUST punish us. Failure to do so would cause Him to contradict his holy and just character. Think about it: Could you worship a holy and perfect God who didn't punish what goes against His nature? It would counter His very being. That's like a court judge who totally dismisses every criminal that steps foot in their courtroom – deeming everyone "not guilty", despite clear evidence that shows otherwise. Would this judge be considered "just"? Absolutely not. Similarly, there must be a consequence for the breaking of God's law. This consequence consists of eternal separation from Him in hell. And because He is perfect and righteous, He has every right to send each and every one of us (who are sinful, unrighteous, and imperfect) to hell. As a result, He is just in declaring each and every one of us guilty of sin.

> *The Lord reigns forever; he has established his throne for judgment. He will judge the world in righteousness; he will govern the peoples with justice. (Psalm 9:7-8)*

3. God is **LOVE.**

By this point, you're probably wondering, "Well why would anyone want to serve a God who sends people to hell? If He is so good, why would He send them there in the first place?" I believe we are asking the wrong question! It isn't 'Why would He send any one to hell?' But instead, 'How does He find it possible to provide a way out? How can God be just and still let guilty sinners into heaven?' The answer is Jesus! This is the exact point where the Gospel (the good news) comes in! But the Gospel holds no value until you have a clear understanding of why you need it in the first place – Why you need a Savior. It's like trying to tell a person with a fatal disease that there is a cure…but there is one problem: they don't know they have the disease and that they're dying. To this person, the cure holds no value. Until they are aware that they possess the disease, and that it will kill them, being informed about a cure means absolutely nothing.

The same applies to you. The disease is known as "Sinfulness." And its result is death – eternal death. But get this, the cure is Jesus. You see, there had to be a "way" for God to administer His wrath against sin without punishing us, but yet still be just. This Way was Jesus Christ. Despite our wickedness, God still saw fit to intervene and send a Savior to bear our punishment, so that we would not have to. He wrapped Himself

11

in flesh, came to Earth, and endured torture on a cross to fulfill the requirement. If this is not love, then I don't know what is. So when we say, "God is love" we are not merely describing his actions – It is WHO HE IS. It is His nature. We often think that the term love in relation to God is looked at as "to embrace or accept." This is not totally true. Love is compassion, and in light of eternity, He saw fit to show such compassion by reconciling us back to Him through Jesus Christ. Now look at John 3:16, perhaps the most known verse in the Bible, and see if it doesn't have a clearer meaning to you.

Whoever does not love does not know God, because God is love. (1 John 4:8)

But God demonstrates his own love for us in this: While we were still sinners, Christ died for us. (Romans 5:8)

At the core of your very being, the most significant aspect of who you are in this life is illustrated by what you think of the Creator of life itself. Addressing this issue of our thoughts of God not only sets the premise to what will further be discussed in this book, but it lays the spiritual foundation on which everything else in your life is built! When this concept is correctly understood, man willingly submits himself to everything he knows God to stand for.

BROKEN BELIEVER

NAME: Unknown (The Samaritan Woman at the Well)

LOCATION: John 4:1-42

BROKEN VERSE: "Come see a man who told me everything I ever did. Could this be the Messiah?" (John 4:29)

DESCRIPTION: On a trip to His home land of Galilee, Jesus goes through a town in Samaria. Tired from his journey, He sits down at a well and meets a Samaritan woman, asking her for a drink of water. Although she is standing face to face with Jesus, she has no idea she is talking to the Son of God. She's totally oblivious to who He is and why He is there. After she questions Jesus' request for a drink, Jesus replies, "If you knew the gift of God and who it is that asks you for a drink, you would have asked him and he would have given you living water" (v. 10). This makes me wonder how many of us, due to our unfamiliarity with God, are missing out on His gift that He wants to impart in us. They continue talking and Jesus makes some statements about her life that a normal stranger wouldn't know. She makes a 'Who are You really?' type of statement, saying "Sir...I can see that you are a prophet." But what she didn't realize was that Jesus was more than a prophet. He was God in the flesh. The Messiah. And once Jesus finally reveals this to her, she leaves her water jar and runs and tells the people back in her town! We often wonder and question who God is and what He is like. But once you find out, who are YOU running and telling?

CHAPTER 2

NOT EASILY BROKEN

"We are either in the process of resisting God's truth or in the process of being shaped and molded by his truth."

Charles Stanley

It is something that is rare in the church today. Hearts are void of it. They lack a true enduring of the process. But what we fail to realize is how pivotal it is in the life of the believer. What I'm talking about is brokenness. You may have never really heard of it, but my prayer is that you've felt it. Because it is here where cries of "I'm unworthy!" are met by the unfathomable forgiveness of our Lord and Savior.

Brokenness is what creates that feeling of distance and separation between us and the holy God we serve. In the broken state, the heart is consumed by a certain type of grief that sends us to our knees. With opened eyes, we realize how God views our sin and what it has done to us! In seeing God in His holiness, we are made aware of just how unholy we are. We see just how much our sin grieves God, and in equal fashion, we are grieved over it as well. Have you experienced this? Have you fallen so deeply in love with God that the very sin that breaks His heart also breaks yours?

There are many who claim to be Christians, but have never really understood the weight their sin carries in the eyes of God. They are unaware of it because they've never encountered Him to begin with. The true believer is broken to the core by the realization that his iniquity rips at the heart of God. They are further broken by the comprehension that it constitutes punishment from a righteous and just God – eternal damnation.

15

However, in this state is where we are also marveled by God's prolific mercy and grace. He does not reject our passionate cries of repentance. He does not despise our broken heart. He receives it gladly.

The sacrifices of God are a broken spirit; A broken and a contrite heart, O God, You will not despise. (Psalm 51:17)

Those are the words of David, who expresses one of the most vivid depictions of brokenness in the Bible. In 2 Samuel 12, after committing adultery with Bathsheba and having her husband killed, we see how David's sorrow is accompanied by days of fasting and intimate moments of consecration. He spends nights lying on the ground, pleading with God. His cries for forgiveness are eventually met with reassurance of God's mercy. Isn't this amazing? The same brokenness that brings forth that feeling of separation from God ultimately draws us near to Him. It draws us closer than we've ever been before! We are carried into His loving arms by the atonement made on the cross by Jesus Christ. It isn't until you understand His wrath against sin that you develop an endless appreciation for the sacrifice He made to spare you from it. This is the beautiful privilege of having a true relationship with God. But it is first conceived out of a fearful and reverential view of Him.

THE FEAR OF GOD

Fear God. This is not a popular phrase in our society. It is not widely mentioned in our conversations, nor is it taught in many of our churches. Do you want to know something, though? It is in the Bible. I know you might be thinking, "But Kyle, that's not New Testament teaching. That's the God of the Old Testament, who people were told to fear because He was angry and wrathful during that time." While that is partly true, it is holistically false. How is it that we somehow think that God has changed? As if the nature of His character was altered from the book of Malachi to the book of Matthew? The fear of God is prevalent in the New Testament, and should be just as present in our day. Jesus himself advises to maintain a fear of the Lord. He says in Luke 12:5, "But I will show you whom you should fear: Fear him, who after the killing of the body, has power to throw you into hell. Yes, I tell you, fear him."

We must start with the fear of God before we truly understand the other aspects of His character. It is the foundation of all spiritual knowledge. The Bible says in Proverbs 9:10, "The fear of the LORD is the beginning of wisdom, and knowledge of the Holy One is understanding." This fear must be acquired before you can gain total appreciation for the grace of God. A grace that does not include a reverential fear of God is a false grace.

So, what does it mean to fear God? That's a frequently asked question. I, myself used to wonder, "Does that mean that I should be scared of God?" It's important that we get this right, because it is an essential component of being broken. Let's kill any misconceptions, and establish biblically what it means to fear the Lord:

Scared: A common question that is proposed in relation to the fear of God is, "Does that mean that we are to literally be afraid of God? Should we be scared of Him?" While the terms "scared" and "afraid" are indeed synonyms associated with fear in our day, our relationship with God should not consist of us being afraid of Him. As believers, we have no reason to be scared of God. This is not saying that we are to treat Him informally, with no respect for His capabilities. It doesn't mean that we dismiss His holy character. Instead, it is a reminder that the believer should walk confidently in the promises of the Lord. God has promised believers that nothing can separate us from His love (Romans 8:38-39). Even during situations where it appears that God is disciplining us, we should not allow such circumstances to create a false sense of fright. A sincere relationship with God produces a desire for the believer to draw closer to Him, not push him away in terror.

We are assured by how approachable He is, and how secure we are in Him. Jesus says in John 6, "All that the Father gives me will come to me, and whoever comes to me I will never drive away" (v. 37). He desires for us to come to Him. Not only that, His will is that we remain in Him! It's difficult to do this in the mindset of being scared of God. So we can dismiss any notions that fear equates to being afraid, if you are indeed in Christ Jesus.

Two Words: If we aren't to be afraid of God, how else then should we describe this word fear? When biblically referring to the fear of God, two words accurately define this expression: reverence and awe. Reverence means to have a deep respect and honor in regards to how you treat someone. Likewise, awe is an overwhelming feeling of respect and wonder. While respect is the common denominator of both descriptions, it's important to emphasize what is meant by respect. It is not the casual respect that is shown between us as humans. No, the respect for God constitutes awe and admiration for who He is. It is a conscious awareness that God is both holy and present. The reverential fear of God is only developed by seeing God for who He really is. When you understand who God is – that He is holy, that He is just, and that He is righteous – the way you conduct yourself is then shifted to surround this realization. You no longer see Him as just some graceful, accepting spiritual being who tolerates your bad behavior. You actually are in awe of His holiness and mindful of His wrath. As the believer views God in this wonder for His righteousness, he is humbled. This is what lies on the other side of the bridge of brokenness – humility. The reverence for God breaks our conceited hearts and leads to true humility. We are grounded by the understanding that He is superior and we are inferior. It sends us running towards Him, never wanting to be separated from His majestic presence! As long as your heart is hardened and unperceptive, it is closed to seeing the holiness of God. Ask Him to break it!

Additionally, let's make one thing clear: The holiness of God is something that we actually should tremble at! I say that because it is evident in the Bible. In Isaiah's vision of the Lord, he found himself so unworthy of seeing God, saying *"Woe to me! I am ruined! For I am a man of unclean lips, and I live among a people of unclean lips, and my eyes have seen the King, the LORD Almighty" (Isaiah 6:5)*. Humility at it's highest degree! Isaiah had such a reverence for God that he realized he was in no way worthy of seeing the Lord. He understood how sinful he was in comparison to a perfect God. Feeling undeserving, he trembled at the sight of Him. Likewise in the book of Revelation, John fell at the Lord's feet when he saw Him. *"When I saw him, I fell at his feet as though dead..." (Revelation 1:17)*. I must ask: Do we have this same disposition today? What comes to your mind at the thought of God's supreme holiness? Furthermore, does the holiness of God govern your thinking and behavior? This is what fearing the Lord is about. As we're drawn to Him, we become more and more like Him. What He hates, you hate as well – including sin.

18

To fear the Lord is to hate evil; I hate pride and arrogance, evil behavior and perverse speech. (Proverbs 8:13)

Not applicable: As previously stated, many believe that fearing God is something that is only relevant in the Old Testament. They believe that this teaching does not apply to us today. This is often attributed to God appearing to be more wrathful in the Old Testament than in the New Testament. We read in the O.T. how people were swallowed up by the ground, struck dead for touching the Ark of Covenant, and wiped out by a flood because of God's wrath. This causes many to have a fearful view of the "Old Testament God." So we automatically associate fearing God with being afraid of His wrathful capabilities during that time. Sadly, it's misapprehension. God does not change. He is the same yesterday, today, and forever. The New Testament is filled with commands to fear the Lord. The truth is, we're entreated to do so our whole time here on this earth!

Since you call on a Father who judges each man's work impartially, live out your lives as strangers here in reverent fear. (1 Peter 1:17)

Peter instructs us to live out our time in reverent fear! This means that our entire lifetime should be spent revering the same holy God from the Old Testament, from now until we get to heaven. It is an ongoing process. Paul says, "…continue to work out your salvation with fear and trembling" (Philippians 2:12). In our relationship with God, fear is an aspect that must remain constant. It is continuous. The reverence for God is a motive for not turning away from Him, because we know that there is terror outside of His presence. Seek Him with your whole heart, and the spirit of the fear of the Lord will consume you. It is a clear and undeniable consciousness that is vital to the broken believer. Ask yourself, "Do I really fear God? More importantly, do my daily actions reflect this?" We aren't easily broken, due to our pride. But once broken, we're easily humbled. I can't stress enough how significant this is. Continuously get in the presence of the Almighty Lord, pleading that you never lose your wonder for Him!

TURNING

"Repent" is another word that is not favorable in our society. It has such a harsh connotation attached to it. Immediate feelings of guilt and judgement can surface from hearing it. I'll be honest, when I used to hear or read that word, all I heard was "SINNER!" (in the most aggressive manner) screamed at me. But instead of viewing this term as being condemned and forced to change, you must see it as a significant action that brings you closer to God.

Many view repentance as a feeling of sorrow. But it's much more than that. To repent means to "change one's mind." This changing of the mind is in relation to who Christ is. It's impossible to totally place your faith in Jesus without changing your mind about who He is and what He has done. It then results in a turning from what you once saw as acceptable. It literally requires you to turn around and walk in the other direction; turning to God as supremely valuable and away from everything else as invaluable. Fundamentally, repentance is a shifting of the values of the soul. But as long as we maintain a view of rejection, our hearts will never be broken.

I know, it's easy to take things personal and defend ourselves when it comes to our sin. We tend to feel judged whenever we're called out on it. In a heartbeat, we'll even quote the Bible (often times out of context) in an attempt to combat our accuser. "Don't judge me. The Bible says, 'Don't judge!' "Translation – "Shut up and let me sin in peace!" I understand, no one likes to be confronted about their hangups and bad habits. It's not the most comfortable position to be in. But conviction isn't supposed to make us comfortable. And while there is a certain approach that should be taken when confronting others about sin (doing so with grace and love), there's also one that should be taken when being confronted about it.

I must pose the question: Could there be a reason why you're so defensive about your sin? Maybe it's because you actually enjoy it, but are unaware of how detrimental it is in your life? Tim Keller once said, "The sin that is most destructive in your life right now is the one you are most defensive about." Think about that. What sin are you most protective over? What sin do you find yourself making excuses for? Even more, is it something that you have just grown to accept? It's easy for us to embrace our iniquity and fall into the lie of "It's just who I am." However, the Holy Spirit doesn't call us to embrace sin. He calls us to overcome it. The world encourages us to welcome who we are and accept our sin nature. Jesus encourages us to welcome who HE is, so that He can deliver us from it. He meets us right where we are, but loves us too much to leave us there. We prevent ourselves from allowing this to happen when we reject correction and close our hearts to truth.

I used to struggle with this. As a child, I often fought correction. This defiance crept into my spiritual life as I grew older. I never wanted to accept that the lifestyle I was living was considered sinful. And the moment I was challenged on it, even from reading the bible, I got defensive. There was no way I could confess that I actually enjoyed certain sin in my life. Eventually, I grew to accept my sin. And the most difficult reality for me to face was that the sin I enjoyed so much was pulling me further away from God. Unaware of this, I justified my actions. Whether it was pre-marital sex or indulging in excessive drinking, I was the king of finding ways to excuse my behavior. "I'm a man, this is the way I'm supposed to be. I was wired this way. God knows I love Him, He understands." I had set up camp in the town of Sinville and would not allow myself to be moved.

Things started to change one night when my girlfriend (now wife) made the challenge of all challenges. We were nearing the end of our college careers and had been dating for about 5 years at this point. One evening, we were talking on the phone, having a good conversation. All of a sudden, it went south when she made a random comment.

"Kyle, we need to talk about something."

"Ok……" I replied. I was really thinking, "Uh oh." If you know like I know, these words can change the whole dynamic of a conversation. They often mean that the conversation is about to get serious. A million things started racing through my mind as I wondered what could be wrong that caused her to suddenly make that statement. Nothing could have prepared me for what was said next.

"I want us to stop having sex."

Talk about mood killer. She might as well have said, "Kyle, you're a terrible person. I've made a mistake by being with you. Kill yourself." That's pretty much how I interpreted her comment. Feelings of confusion, guilt, and frustration consumed me all at one time. Immediately, I got defensive and began questioning her.

"Where is this coming from? Why? What did I do?" I replied.

She responded by saying, "What we're doing isn't right. We're not married. God isn't pleased with it, and you know that."

Honestly, I didn't. I wasn't even looking to see if He cared. At that point, I had become so numb to sexual sin that it was normal to me. Everyone did it, and I figured that us being in love gave us a pass to engage in what we would continue to do in marriage. In my mind, I was setting us up for a future of intimacy.

I didn't take this too well. I was upset because I felt like she was directly confronting me about something I enjoyed so much. I took it personal, as if she thought she was some holy Saint looking down on me. I felt judged. But all of this was out of pure misunderstanding. After more questions and some debate, I eventually gave in. I agreed to it, but for all the wrong reasons. I determined in my mind to be celibate until marriage in order to show Bri that I really loved her, instead of determining in my heart to be celibate to show God that I really loved Him. Initially, it was a half-hearted pledge rather than a loving commitment to honor God.

As time went on though, I began to grow in Christ. I started spending time alone with Him, reading His word and developing a genuine relationship with Him. Over time, the scales were removed from my eyes and I started gaining understanding. I grew to understand that He was the Creator of this beautiful act of intimacy, and that it's ultimately something good that was designed to have purpose. I no longer wanted to displease Him by engaging in sex outside of His wonderful design. I sincerely wanted to turn from what I once saw as valuable, and allow my love for Him to empower me in purity. This repentance was key in my walk with Christ. It wasn't easy, but I can now look back and sincerely say it was one of the best decisions my wife and I ever made. I thank God for using Bri to grab my attention and inducing me to fully submit to Him.

TRULY REPENTANT OR JUST SORRY?

I can speak for many when I say that we would much rather continue in our immorality than be challenged and encouraged to turn from it. We're okay with it, as long as it doesn't lead us to destruction; As long as there are no consequences. Our goal as followers of Christ should not be to just escape the consequences of sin, but to escape our love for it altogether!

Remember this: God's allowance of your sin does not mean that He approves of it. As a culture, we have somehow manufactured in our minds the idea that because the consequences of our sins aren't immediate, that they're acceptable. I'm confident in saying that sin would be a lot less appealing if the penalty for it was instant. But thankfully, we serve a God who is patient and merciful. We are given free will, but we are also given a way of escape. Escape from what? Romans 6:23 says, *"For the wages of sin is death..."* This is the penalty of our sin – death (eternal separation from God). All it takes though is for us to continue reading that scripture to gain insight to God's merciful provision, *"...but the gift of God is eternal life in Christ Jesus our Lord."* This is our way of escape; our way out from the eternal punishment due to us.

You might have heard that time and time again, but being broken results in putting total belief in this Way of escape; So much that you're not just apologetic about your sin, but that you fully desire to turn from it. There's a difference between being sorry ABOUT your sin (worldly sorrow), and being repentant (turning from it).

Godly sorrow brings repentance that leads to salvation and leaves no regret, but worldly sorrow brings death. (2 Corinthians 7:10)

It's important to know that not all sorrow signifies true repentance. I've been in the position after doing something I knew was wrong, and quickly asking God for forgiveness. I often treated God's grace like a "Get Out of Jail Free" card. Many times, I knew beforehand that what I was preparing to do was wrong, but engaged in it anyway. "I'll just ask God to forgive me afterwards." Paul says this type of worldly sorrow brings death. Genuine Godly sorrow results in change, and not just remorseful thoughts. It is a changed attitude toward sin itself. Through Godly sorrow, the heart is changed. And where the heart is changed, life is changed! Personally, I had to ask God to give me a desire to turn from the sin that appeared to entangle me. My meager requests for forgiveness had to be replaced with proactive requests to be reformed – "God help me develop a disgust for the sin that I know You died to deliver me from." My prayer is that we aren't just sorry about our sin and it's consequences, but that we truly seek to turn from it. You'll be broken to believe that you can indeed be renewed by Jesus!

BROKEN BELIEVER

NAME: David

LOCATION: 2 Samuel 11 &12

BROKEN VERSE: The sacrifices of God are a broken spirit; A broken and a contrite heart, O God, You will not despise (Psalm 51:17)

DESCRIPTION: David was a man after God's own heart. But we see that even those who follow God are subject to the stumbling blocks of evil. Not only does David commit adultery, but he uses his political power to cover up his sin. David's response however is what is really worth emulating. He is quite grieved over his shameful actions. His confession, "I have sinned against the Lord" (2 Samuel 12:13) is followed by repentant nights lying in sackcloth and fasting. His heart is truly broken and he seeks restoration. Let us be reminded that none of us are immune to the grappling effects of temptation, no matter how strong we think we are. Totally rely on Christ's strength. More importantly, let us always look for the promptings of the Holy Spirit, so we don't learn from David's lessons the hard way.

CHAPTER 3

"I Still Get Jealous."

"Idols are not bad things. They're good things which you're looking to, to give you what only God can give you."

Tim Keller

As I stand at the end of the aisle, my heart begins to race with excitement. I told everyone up to this point that I wasn't going to be nervous. Nor would I cry. I was about to take one of the biggest steps imaginable – marriage. I remember standing next to my pastor in front of a church packed with family and friends. Seeming like the longest 5 minutes of my life, I await my bride. People are smiling and crying, some I had never seen before in my entire life. Music is now playing, and all I can think about is quickly getting this ceremony over with. I longed to officially be one with the person who had endured and sacrificed so much up to this point. Suddenly, those back doors fly open and the most beautiful woman I've ever seen comes into view, dressed in all white and standing arm in arm with her father. She elegantly glides down the aisle, and now all I can think of is how I am about to make a commitment to honor, cherish, and protect this woman until the day I die. Excitement had turned into seriousness, masked with a smile. Then they finally came. The vows! This is the moment of truth. It is my turn to answer. At this point my pastor sounds like the teacher from Charlie Brown, as I gaze into her stunning eyes. All I can think about is her.

"Do you promise to love her, WAH WA-WAH WAH better or for worse, for WA-WAH WAH WAH, in sickness and health, and...." Charlie Brown's teacher is in the background, and I'm still gazing, paralyzed by her beauty and eager to start this new life. All of the sudden, the next

25

few words strike me like a bullet. Charlie Brown's teacher suddenly became what sounded like God himself, clear and distinct as ever. **"FORSAKING ALL OTHERS, BE FAITHFUL ONLY TO HER, FOR AS LONG AS YOU BOTH SHALL LIVE?"**

Hold on. Forsaking all others? Faithful? Only to her? FOR AS LONG AS WE BOTH SHALL LIVE? Jesus! Now, I wasn't afraid of commitment in any way. Nor did I have concerns about my ability to remain faithful to my wife. That was not the issue. But unlike many, I knew the weight that those words carried, especially before God. This is the part of marriage vows that is broken by men and women all over the world. The prevalence of infidelity is destroying marriages daily, partly because many people don't truly view their vows through the eyes of God. What do these words mean? They are a promise to have eyes for my wife, and my wife only. They represent my declaration that no matter what form of enticement I may face, I will forever take seriously the love I claim to have for her. This would be proven by my actions, honoring the sacred covenant that was established on this day. Hopefully you caught the most vital part of that last sentence – "proven by my actions."

Marriage is frequently used in the bible to describe the relationship between God and His people. Biblically, the church is often referred to as the bride, and Jesus as the bridegroom. However, we have a history of not being able to "forsake all others, and be faithful only to Him." To this day, we tend to enamor ourselves with acts of adultery, cheating on God with cheap substitutes. This disloyalty is rooted in the hearts of God's people all throughout the Bible, as the LORD uses infidelity to depict their unfaithful behavior. He describes them as adulterers, and even uses the whole book of Hosea to portray His view of this relationship, equating the people of Israel to a prostitute.

In the Old Testament, God repeatedly ordered the Israelites not to worship anything or anyone other than Himself. He established a covenant, first through Abraham, then through Moses that required their uncompromising love and worship. God was preparing to lead them to The Promised Land. This territory was already inhabited by people who worshipped false gods, such as Baal and Ashtoreth. In their quest to conquer this land and reside in areas containing false gods, The LORD gave them explicit instructions regarding this matter: *"You shall not bow down to them or worship them; for I, the LORD your God, am a jealous God..." (Exodus 20:5).* Doing so would be considered idolatry. And man did these people involve themselves in it! Throughout the Old Testament, we see God's people blatantly disregard God's command and fulfill their selfish desires, being influenced to deviate from the one true God who brought them out of Egypt. The Israelites took it upon themselves to construct man-made idols, bow down to images, and make sacrifices to false gods. They even offered their own children at times, burning them as human sacrifices. We consequently see God's jealousy expressed, and His wrath poured out as punishment for their disobedience. After years of warnings from the prophets, pleading with them to turn back, God ultimately plans for them to be executed, exiled, and the city of Jerusalem destroyed... A jealous God!

In order to fully understand the seriousness of idolatry, we must first break down what an idol is. As previously mentioned, idols for the people of Israel were man-made images and objects that were worshipped as gods. These were frequently wooden or stone carvings, sometimes in the image of animals. Ultimately, these idols drew their attention away from the LORD. Similarly, an idol in modern culture is anything that replaces God in your life. You're probably saying to yourself, "That's crazy. Nothing comes before God in MY life. He's my everything!" I'm sorry to inform you that proof of this goes far beyond your little social media bio that says, "God First." All we have to do is look at your life and determine what is receiving more of your time, and more of your attention than God; anything you place more value on is an idol. It's a false god, and this is evident by how your time is spent and what specifically you indulge in.

TV: Do you spend more time in front of the television than you do reading your bible? Think about it: You have most likely structured your living room furniture in a way that everyone can sit around your television and worship that god. At work, your conversations with co-workers are filled with the juicy details of last night's episode of that show that entertains you with infidelity and murder. I know Christians who get more excited on the day of the week their favorite TV show comes on than they do about getting in the very presence of God. You might be thinking, "Come on, it's not that deep. You're overreacting." But God takes idolatry seriously.

Don't try to minimize the seriousness of yours, thinking it will lighten His view of it.

Career: Do you spend long hours at work, striving for that promotion or seeking to please your boss? No matter how we try to justify this with wanting a better life for ourselves and our family, the core of it is selfish ambition that leads to placing trust in more money and less faith in the ultimate Provider. You are kneeling at the altar of Corporate America, worshiping the gods of status, power, and monetary freedom.

Success: Are you so determined to become successful, that you'll do almost anything and everything to accomplish your goals? Chasing such things can lead to distraction. Your time is spent planning how you can prosper yourself, rather than seeking to be prospered by God so you can be used by Him. Listen, there's no success apart from commitment to Jesus Christ. Contrary to what many believe, it's the only thing that matters! Your longing desire for earthly success could be the very thing that leads you to eternal failure.

Sports: Are you more enthused when your favorite sports team is playing than you are when worshipping God? Do your conversations regarding your fantasy football team get more attention and energy from you than Jesus on Sundays? You jump, shout, and scream during the game with evidence that this brings you excitement. Your true god is displayed as you stand and clap for touchdowns, but sit in silence during praise and worship at church. Some people will excuse their non-emotionalism with declarations of, "I love God, but that clapping and singing stuff is just not who I am." Well I can honestly declare that one of the clear marks of the Christian life is the joy and delight we express in the mere thought of our Lord and Savior; let alone when offered an opportunity to praise Him. If you're too cool to worship God in public here on Earth, you definitely will struggle if you make it to heaven. Because that is exactly what your time in paradise will be spent doing, praising our holy God nonstop, over and over and over again. It's not just about praise and worship though, it's about where your passion truly is overall!

Significant other: Do you place more value on trying to please your significant other than pleasing God? Yes, your spouse can be an idol. Your boyfriend or girlfriend can be an idol. As you desire so badly to satisfy them, you exalt them to a place in your heart above God. I'm not at all saying that service isn't important in our marriages and relationships. Our love should certainly be shown by our actions. I'm a firm believer in spouses trying to out-love each other with acts of kindness and affection. The problem arises though when you seek their approval and affirmation over God's; Their time, over time with Him; and solely finding security in them, rather than resting in the comfort of Jesus. All the while, they are leading you further and further from Christ. Many people deny that this is taking place in their relationship. But one thing is for sure: If they aren't leading you TO Him, they're leading you astray – an idol.

These are only a handful of false gods that have us claiming to follow the LORD, but expressing otherwise in our actions. Let's not get into technology – Tablets that keep us consumed and cell phones that have our faces buried in screens, wasting hours upon hours concerning ourselves with the lives of other people. Inherently these things aren't bad within themselves. I'm not saying there's anything wrong with watching television, having a job, working hard, or liking sports. Believe me, I like to think I am a hard worker, and as a former college athlete, I like my fair share of sports. But we take what is essentially good (family, people, jobs, work ethic, intimacy, etc.), and we deify them. We make them ultimate things in our lives. The result is us living for them, and not for God.

Let's refer back to my wedding ceremony. When I stood at that altar and agreed to honor those vows, I essentially settled in my heart that I belong to my wife and my wife only. We were now going to be one flesh, and I had to be willing to abandon anything that would attempt to draw me away from her. Likewise, when we agree to follow Christ, we are giving a solid commitment to surrender our whole selves to Him – our time, our money, our marriage, our life! We will discuss what this specifically looks like later. However, it is vital to realize how quick we are to say with our mouths, "God comes first" but our devotion to temporal things of this world proves otherwise.

HEART CHECK

The issue of idolatry is fundamentally an issue of the heart. In no way am I attempting to persuade you to desert everything in your life and become a monk. Instead, I'm asking you to thoroughly determine where your heart truly lies by examining what gets the most of it! Jesus reminds us of this, as He commanded His disciples not to store their treasures on earth but in heaven. The heart issue is affirmed as he exclaims, *"For where your treasure is, there your heart will be also." (Matthew 6:21)*

When we think of treasure, we think of value. We think of worth. Where is your treasure? Where do you find your sense of worth? Is it in material possessions? Is it in the validation of your social media followers? Is it in your career? Or is it exclusively in the unconditional love of Jesus Christ? If your heart truly resides in Jesus, a majority of your time is spent pursuing Him, and not things that ultimately have no eternal value. You long to be in the comfort of His presence, rather than submerging yourself in worldly pleasures.

Not only is your heart revealed by what you pursue, it is also shown by what you say; what you talk about. *"...for out of the overflow of the heart the mouth speaks." (Matthew 12:34).* The words that come out of your mouth are a verbal depiction of what's in your heart! Have you ever stopped to think about that? No matter how much you claim to love Jesus, your words call your bluff. That same tongue you use to praise God, is also used to swear, gossip, lie, and curse people. What do your words say about your heart? Do they illustrate your love for Jesus? It is quite possible that this is a direct result of what you're consuming. If you are feeding yourself things that aren't pleasing to God (explicit music/tv shows/books), such language will naturally come out in your talk. These things subconsciously settle in your mind. Soon, the content begins to permeate your heart, and before you know it, you are speaking the very filth that you continuously spend time consuming. But the more time we spend at the feet of Jesus, ingesting His Word and asking Him to make us more like Him, the more He begins to renovate our behavior, our language, and our desires!

PRAY

I want to challenge you at this very moment to do something that you're probably not expecting. Put this book down and pray. Now? Yes, that's right, now. If you're at home, go to a secluded place and get on your face. If you're in a coffee shop, put this book down, bow your head, and spill it all out. Have an honest conversation with God about your idolatry. Tell Him about that boyfriend or girlfriend that you have allowed to take

His place. How you have made THEM your god. Confess your worship of status and power. Ask Him to break you of your infatuation with that TV show that glorifies adultery, and doesn't glorify Him! If we are honest with ourselves, we all have false gods that are overriding our hearts. So do not try to convince yourself that this part does not apply to you. I'm not sure what that idol is for you; what you have been giving more time and attention to than God. But now that it has been acknowledged, I pray the Holy Spirit has convicted and compelled you to withdraw somewhere and seek forgiveness. God is jealous for you! Cry out to Him with a contrite heart, and ask Him to remove anything that is blocking you from solely desiring Him. This is part of being broken. DO IT!

THE GOD OF SELF

Innately, the cause of modern idolatry is one thing – self. We love ourselves. This isn't a simple matter of being confident. Rather, its an obsession; An obsession that causes us to overestimate our view of who we are. While we no longer bow down to idols and images of the Old Testament, we do launch ourselves at the altar of Me. We are a culture obsessed with taking "selfies" that flood social media, and reading self-help books that line bookstore shelves. It is apparent that we have become a people totally fixated on how we look, what others think of us, and what we can do for ourselves. Well-known Christian evangelist, Billy Graham, once said, "Our idolatry is very unique in our day because we worship ourselves." This couldn't be any closer to the truth.

I've met people who claim to be "Self-made." They reside in a deceptive world of self-reliance, and take pride in their self-sufficient ability. Their own claims of authority have eclipsed their view of the Lord's sovereignty. However, they fail to understand that they don't have the intellect to establish themselves. It is only God, the Creator and Sustainer, who possesses the knowledge and power to do so. And as quickly as He can elevate you in this life, He can also take away.

What's more frightening is society's tendency to abide by our self-established morals. We have made our own selves idols, stemming our views of morality from what *we* feel. For the sake of this book, we will call this idol "iGod." Here, every thought and behavior originates from "I." The iGod says, "I do what I want. I say what I want. And I deserve whatever

31

I desire. It's my life." In this state, you believe your standards permit you to think and act any way you please. You are not accountable to anyone. This is an extremely dangerous mindset to have! It's dangerous because you have essentially claimed yourself to be Almighty God, replacing His standards with your own. This results in hopeless subjectivity regarding good and evil. Whatever you feel is right is right, and whatever you feel is wrong is wrong. It allows you to be easily influenced as well. So whatever becomes socially acceptable in culture (pre-marital sex, marijuana, homosexual marriage, etc), most likely becomes acceptable to you as well.

The iGod is what drives us toward immorality. It's an egotistic matter of the heart that leads us to indulge in sinful behavior. Its selfishness; and **selfishness is the root of all sin**. This is when self is the center of your life. Whether it's viewing pornography or stealing, selfishness causes us to do whatever we feel is necessary to satisfy our wants. The source of every divorce is someone's selfish tendencies; whether the divorce is due to financial disagreement, lack of affection, or adultery. Selfishness is the truth behind every lie told. It is the driving force behind greed. And it pushes us to desire the very things that distance us from God. However, the person who takes this Christian life seriously discovers freedom from being centered in him or herself.

Selfishness entices us to place ourselves above others, and furthermore, above God. Rather than thinking about the effect our sin can have on others, we live in the moment, focusing solely on the temporary pleasure that sin gives us. Have you ever stopped to think about who else your sin is affecting? – family, friends, strangers? Have you thought about the long lasting effect it could have years down the road on your grandchildren? The habits you're practicing and the life you're modeling now could potentially get passed down to your family generations from now. Have you reflected upon how your selfishness has direct and indirect consequences for you and others? It is not just about you.

HEART CHECK #2

Again, this selfishness issue is tied directly to your heart. Jesus indicates that the heart is wicked, and everything we do flows from it. In Matthew 15, the Pharisees attempt to catch Jesus on a religious technicality when they spot His disciples eating with unwashed hands – a practice that went against a common tradition of the elders. They ask Jesus as the leader of this group of people to explain their actions. Jesus' response throws everyone for a loop. Like He regularly did in His ministry, Jesus replies by shifting the focus from the minor issue to the bigger picture. He informs them that it's not what goes into someone's mouth that defiles them, but what comes out. Rather than focusing on eating with unwashed hands and following their man-made traditions, He implores them to search within to see what is truly contaminating them. When explaining this to the disciples, He clarifies that this contamination is an issue of the heart, and not the hands! The selfishness of the heart is the source of a person's immoral behavior – both words and actions.

> *"Are you still so dull?" Jesus asked them. "Don't you see that whatever enters the mouth goes into the stomach and then out of the body? But the things that come out of the mouth come from the heart, and these make a man 'unclean.' For out of the heart come evil thoughts, murder, adultery, sexual immorality, theft, false testimony, slander.* (Matthew 15:16-19)

Jesus clearly states that it doesn't matter what your sin is, it is directly linked to one thing – your heart. What has your selfishness driven you to engage in? Jesus is asking you to search yourself. He wants you to let Him expose those impure motives pushing you toward sin. He then wants to replace them with an everlasting thirst for holiness, which can be administered only by Him.

BEAUTIFULLY JEALOUS

God hates our adultery. He despises our extramarital enthusiasm towards activities and people that have replaced Him in our hearts. This jealousy isn't just part of his character, it is who He is – "...*for the LORD, whose name is Jealous, is a jealous God." (Exodus 34:14)*. The Bible says His name is Jealous, and while this may seem harsh, it is actually a wonderful assurance. God's jealousy beautifully shows His love for us, despite our wondering ways. And it's amazing to know that He is jealous for our love; jealous for our trust; jealous for our company! Overall, The LORD is jealous for your heart, and He's continuously battling for it. However, He refuses to contend as you willingly recruit these idols for Him to compete against.

BROKEN BELIEVER

NAME: Zacchaeus (the Tax Collector)

LOCATION: Luke 19:1-10

BROKEN VERSE: "…Look, Lord! Here and now I give half of my possessions to the poor…" (Luke 19:8)

DESCRIPTION: Zacchaeus was a chief tax collector. You must understand that tax collectors didn't have a favorable reputation during this time. They were seen as wicked and sinful. But he was a man so determined to see who Jesus is, that he climbs a tree to see over the crowd and view Him. The Bible also states that Zacchaeus was quite wealthy. However, we see such a brokenness in him that he tells Jesus, "Look, Lord! Here and now I give half of my possessions to the poor, and if I have cheated anybody out of anything, I will pay back four times the amount." Zacchaeus is a transformed witness who detaches himself from his money to prove that he wholeheartedly wants to follow Jesus! What idols are you willing to detach yourself from to do the same?

CHAPTER 4

SUICIDE

"The world's philosophy says live for self, but God's word says DIE TO SELF"

Unknown

As a child, I used to love going to the grocery store with my mother. I took pride in being her helper. Glancing at the grocery list to see what the next item was, I would sprint down the aisles to quickly find it for her. "Here it is, Mom!" I would yell, as I grabbed it and put it in the cart. Of course sometimes (more like most of the time) it would be the wrong brand or size. So I had to take the item back. I also loved to push the cart. She would allow me to do so occasionally, until I started accidentally clipping the back of her heels as she walked in front of me. She hated when I did that.

The overall experience was great, aside from one thing: I could never get what I wanted! Before we even entered the store she would grab my arm, bend down, look me square in the eyes and say, "Kyle, I want you to hear me loud and clear. When we get in this store, do not ask for anything because I'm not getting you anything. No candy, no chips, no toys…. NOTHING." I'd agree and follow my mom into the store, staring at the other kids who had fruit snacks piled up in their carts and new action figures in their hands. Meanwhile, I was being told to suppress my wants out of obedience. At the time, I never understood this. "I can't get ANYthing?" I would think to myself, too afraid to actually ask out loud. I thought it was just my mom being my mom. Other times, I attributed it to financial struggles. I would wonder, "Are we doing that bad? I can't even get a pack of gum?"

35

I soon found out that this wasn't the case at all though. It wasn't that my mom couldn't afford to buy me anything. We weren't in any type of financial hardship. She was actually trying to teach me something. She wanted me to know that although I might want something, I don't NEED it; that not all things are good for me. Most importantly, my mom knew that whatever she would get for me at the store only satisfied me for a short period of time. A pack of Skittles would only gratify me during the car ride home, then I would be asking for ice cream. A new action figure would entertain me for the rest of the day, but tomorrow it would no longer be fun to play with. It was a reoccurring theme of dissatisfaction. Sound familiar? My mom was attempting to instill in me the discipline required for self-control. She knew me. She knew the more I indulged, the more I desired. I quickly learned to forfeit what Kyle wanted, for what my mom knew was in my best interest. To no surprise, this same lesson applies in our relationship with Jesus. For me in those days it was something simple like candy, but let us apply this concept to any teenager or adult – because our desires don't go away as we age, they just breed a hunger for deeper forms of sin. I want you to replace the "candy" with any type of familiar sin – fornication, substance abuse, greed, drunkenness, pride, etc. Temporarily harness it, as we will come back to it later. We must first discuss the action that must take place in deciding to follow Jesus.

OPERATION: DEATH?

Death is something that many of us don't like to think about. But what if I told you this was necessary to follow Jesus? What if I told you that the solution to your "selfishness problem" is suicide? I know that suicide is never the right answer to any problem we face, but I'm not talking about taking your physical life. This isn't about a physical death. Rather, it is an internal one – carnal suicide. This suicide requires you to die…. TO yourself! What does this mean? Well let's grasp an understanding of carnality first. In one sense, carnality refers to the desires and passions of the body. This is partly what needs to die. But in whole, the term "carnal" refers to that which is not spiritual; anything that is worldly or temporal. This part of us must be killed on a daily basis. Paul refers to this in his letter to the people of Galatia, stating, *"Those who belong to Christ Jesus have crucified the flesh with its passions and desires." (Galatians 5:24)*

In terms of following Jesus, how can this death actually be portrayed? I'm reminded of what this looks like through Jesus' own eyes. In Luke 9, He paints a picture regarding what the carnal suicide process looks like for His followers:

> *"If anyone would come after me, he must deny himself and take up his cross daily and follow me."* (Luke 9:23)

Every time I read that passage, I cringe. I cringe because I know what it is asking of me. And if I can be honest, it sometimes scares me. In order to understand what this Scripture exactly means, we must look at the context of this verse. Here is the backdrop: Jesus is with His disciples, and had just requested their opinions of who they thought He was. After praying, he asks them, "Who do the crowds say that I am?" (Luke 9:18). They respond with multiple answers, including John the Baptist, Elijah, and one of the prophets that has risen from the dead. Jesus asks an even more important question - a question that He often asks many of us at a point in our lives: "But what about you? Who do *YOU* say that I am?" (emphasis added). Peter answers, "The Christ of God."

It has now been established who Jesus is – The Christ, or the Messiah, meaning "chosen one" or "deliverer." Jesus had come to save the believers of this world from the penalty of their sins. His purpose was to deliver them to the Father as blameless and pure. After establishing who He is, Jesus enlightens them on what must take place for Him to fulfill this purpose:

> *"The Son of Man must suffer many things and be rejected by the elders, chief priest and teachers of the law, and he must be killed and on the third day be raised to life."* (Luke 9:22)

Jesus foretold what was getting ready to happen to Him - suffering and death. That is what being the Messiah actually entailed. Contrarily, it was in no way what the Jews envisioned of the Messiah, whom they read the prophets speak of in the Scriptures. They were expecting the Messiah to come and overthrow the Roman government that had been controlling them for years. They were awaiting to be set free from Roman oppression. Here Jesus is, however, saying that He is going to be rejected, captured, and killed. Following this statement, He then implies to them that if they truly want to be His disciples, they will have to follow suit and endure the same. For the original Twelve disciples, this meant literal suffering and death. Jesus exclaimed that this is vital in choosing to follow Him. He even explains in detail at one point what they will endure. *"You must be on your guard. You will be handed over to the local councils and flogged in the synagogues. On account of me you will stand before governors and kings as witnesses to them." (Mark 13:9)* But what does this look like for us today? Now that we understand the context, we can interpret what Jesus truly meant when referring to the words deny, take up your cross, and follow!

DENYING

People today despise this. They dislike not being able to have what they want. They disagree when told they should suppress their longings. Since childhood, we've naturally hated being told, "No." But for us as Christians, denial is imperative in our walk with Jesus. Before we jump into this, I want to be clear that this isn't about following a particular set of rules. Nor is denial something that occurs out of fearful obligation. Rather, it is daily submission to the Holy Spirit that is demonstrated out of pure love; A love for Jesus that stems from His love for us on the cross. So as Jesus tells us to deny, He is desiring that our love for Him be so great, that we willingly destroy any part of us that does not look, act, or sound like Him. We are to deny the temptations of sin. We are to deny our flesh – the carnal part of us that desires to go against God. We are to deny ungodliness. We are to deny that little voice that whispers, "I know you WANT to do right, I know you WANT to be pure, I know you WANT to be obedient to God…. but this little bit of sinful pleasure isn't going to hurt. Do it!"

Not only is modern denial the rejection of sinful temptation. It is also the denial of self-centered ambitions. In a world that strokes our egos and encourages us to pursue our wants, Jesus commands His followers to do the exact opposite. He's saying, "Although you want to pursue YOUR earthly goals, I'm calling you to be eternity-minded. I desire for you to live a life that is completely sold out to Me!"

I remember trying to follow Jesus without understanding this command. It didn't work. My life choices were determined by what I felt was right. I chased what I desired. Partying was constant and my tongue was untamed. Additionally, my life goals came first, and I gave God whatever leftover time existed. Sadly, it was all justified in my eyes. I repeatedly defended my actions with conversations like, "God, You understand. You know I'm not perfect." I would vindicate my own ambitious ways with thoughts like, "I'm pursuing my dreams for a better life! There's nothing wrong with that, God." When in fact, there absolutely was something wrong with it. I was intentionally using God's grace and mercy to excuse my life of habitual sin and self-satisfaction. The concept of denial was foreign because I was so Me-conscious. Nothing else mattered. *"I denied myself nothing my eyes desired; I refused my heart no pleasure. My heart took delight in all my work, and this was the reward for all my labor"* (Ecclesiastes 2:10). These are the elements of an unrestrained life; A life that refuses to slay the passionate lusts of the flesh. When you have this mentality, you greenlight whatever type of sin appeases you. You place your aspirations above the will of God, and still attempt to use Him to attain them. Eventually, you are so absorbed by this lifestyle that you become desensitized to the very things pulling you away from Jesus. You become so earthly-minded, that eternity is nowhere in your view. This is what occurs when we don't purpose our hearts to deny. You try to hold on to the desires of the world with one hand, and occasionally reach for God with the other. But see, there is no middle ground! Following Jesus doesn't consist of periodic obedience whenever it's convenient for you. It is all or nothing. Those who refuse to deny, continuing to place their stakes in this life, will end up empty. Jesus says this clearly after his command to deny, take up, and follow:

"For whoever wants to save his life will lose it, but whoever loses his life for me will save it." (Luke 9:24)

Now, am I advising you to completely forfeit all of your hopes and dreams? Of course not. What I am saying is that it is dangerous when those dreams do not stem from Christ to begin with. Why? Because your pursuits and efforts surround your own self, and not Him. Sometimes God actually calls us out of what *we* think is our purpose (or what others have told us our purpose is), and into a life that is truly meant to serve Him. This requires shifting your focus from your personal ambitions, and aligning it solely with His will. There comes a point where you're content with this, because you understand that true joy comes from drawing others closer to Jesus. Understand this: real Christ followers do not use this life to merely satisfy themselves. Instead, they dedicate it to wholeheartedly serving God and other people. Ask yourself, "Does my life reflect this type of commitment? Is what I'm pursuing bringing glory to Jesus Christ?" If not, you have some denying to do. Deny yourself, and examine what areas of self-want in your life can be eradicated and substituted!

CROSS-CARRYING

Jesus also commanded his followers to take up their cross. Many of us are familiar with the symbol of the cross. We see it on top of churches and as pieces of jewelry. We wear it as a fixture around our necks, and even tattoo it on our bodies. We understand the imagery, but don't fully comprehend how to live out its meaning as Christ followers. So let's break it down. The meaning of the cross itself is death. It was an instrument used to torture and kill individuals by means of crucifixion. We frequently forget that Jesus was not the only person killed by being crucified. Not to devalue or discount His sacrifice in any way, but He was not the first nor the last person to be put on a cross to die. It was a common form of execution, believed to have originated from the Persians, and eventually adopted by the Romans. Crucifixion provided a death that was slow and painful (by which we get the word "excruciating"). It was also meant to be humiliating. Occasionally, the convicted individual was stripped and forced to carry the crossbeam to his or her place of execution. Many Galileans were subjected to this by the Romans, and Jesus was no different. We see this in the Bible as He was ruthlessly tortured, then forced to transport His own cross to Calvary.

> Carrying his own cross, he went out to the place of the Skull (which in Aramaic is called Golgotha). (John 19:17)

The Twelve disciples were all too familiar with the meaning of the cross. They were aware of the humiliation and suffering associated with it. They knew it was an instrument that represented one thing – death. So as Jesus was telling them to take up their cross daily, He was actually telling them to be willing to die to follow Him. What does this mean for you? Ironically, nearly 2,000 years later, the message has not changed. Jesus is still imploring you to take up your cross! He is telling you that if you want to follow Him, you must suffer. And it's not farfetched to say that you must die. Your death is a full surrender to Him that brings about pain, humiliation, and discomfort. It requires you to become uncomfortable. You see, it is easy to follow Jesus when life is easy and care-free. But Jesus has not called us to live an easy life. True commitment to Him often brings trials. However, it is a commitment that ultimately results in life! The sacrifice is worth the reward. This is what encourages us to endure what we must — taking up our cross daily for the One who truly loves us. Countless times I've had to ask myself, "Am I truly carrying my cross?" I can honestly say that I've dropped it on occasion. It's heavy. It's burdensome, and I've cried several nights questioning my calling. Tears of insufficiency have left me with doubts about my ability to carry out such a task. But I'm constantly reminded that I'm strengthened by the Holy Spirit to persist. The same Jesus who withstood the beatings, ridicule, and torture now resides within me. I'm empowered by the Almighty to continue dying to ME and living for HIM!

Whether its sin or our quest for success, Jesus makes it very apparent that your life requires death. A killing of your natural self must take place. Your flesh seeks to rebel against holiness, and it must be brought under subjection. How does this take place? As simple as it may sound, it starts with one thing - prayer. This isn't just a vague expression of your sorrow that we're talking about here. It is a sincere cry for help. You must constantly ask God to:

Help you remove anything in your life that isn't pleasing to Him. Impure thoughts, tempting environments, friendships that entice you; these are all influences that can impede on your spiritual progression if not captured and discarded. The first step in carnal suicide is realizing that your pursuit of Jesus is always hindered by your pursuit of sin.

Allow the Holy Spirit to convict, guide, and strengthen you. What does this mean? Part of His job is to empower you! When you are faced with any form of temptation, ask the Holy Spirit to assist you in killing your desires. Yield to His voice.

THE BOTTOM LINE: FOLLOW

Jesus is the One who speaks directly against your self-centered thinking. He is the One instructing you to forfeit what you want, for what He requires. This is probably the most difficult part to accept for any person striving to follow Christ. Not to worry, it was hard for the people in Jesus' day also. Many who started following Him turned away and left.

They determined that the specifics of following Jesus didn't line up with what they were willing to give of themselves (John 6:66).

We see, however, that denying, cross-carrying, and following wasn't simply Jesus requesting a favor. Dying to yourself isn't something that's optional in your Christian walk. Rather, it is a requirement. Taking up your cross is a prerequisite to being a follower of Christ. Jesus doesn't say, "If you want to be my disciple, live life the way you choose, give in to your wants, and get to me in your spare time." It's never portrayed that way in Scripture. He says, "Yes, it's going to be hard. You *will* be persecuted. You *will* be talked about. And yes, you *will* suffer!" But we must always keep in mind that the reward will be so much greater than the suffering that we endure.

Jesus knows that our carnal thinking deters us from completely surrendering ourselves to Him. He cares less about blessing our selfish ambitions, and more about our willingness to sacrifice them for Him. Similar to how my mother knew me as it related to candy and toys, Jesus is all too familiar with your selfishness. Your iGod. Your fleshly desires. He's fully aware that your pursuit of them satisfies you only temporarily. He knows that once you've fulfilled that desire, it won't be long until you're knocking on the door of sin again, asking for more. Ultimately, Jesus is laying the foundational requirements of following Him. He wants you to die to yourself, passing up the pleasures of immorality and embracing the greater riches of His reward.

The dying process requires something that is quite difficult for many people – humility. It is the struggle of discarding the inflated view of ourselves, and totally allowing God to be positioned in our lives as authoritative. A person cannot follow Jesus with a co-pilot attitude. Unfortunately, that is the approach some Christians have. Following Jesus means that you are willing to displace yourself, acknowledging Him as supreme. The closer you get to Jesus, the more you mature and grow in Him. And the more you grow, the more aware you become of how unlike Him you actually are! This is what humility is all about. But naturally, pride gets in the way and tells us we still have a right to be in control; that we can still do, say, and act how we want. It says, "This life is still about me, and I refuse to release total control of it to someone else." The moment you attempt to pursue God while still clinching to your pride, you immediately declare that His will and ways are not sufficient. The remedy to this spiritually unhealthy outlook is understanding, through His word, that God created us for a reason. And this reason involves knowing that His purpose for us surpasses anything that surrounds our individual desires. Self no longer becomes our reason for existing!

Jesus is offering an exchange; a trade-off. Your momentary pleasure for eternal joy. What a proposal! But it's sad that so many people, perhaps yourself included, openly reject this free offer. Instead, they choose to chase their empty passions. Trust me, I've been there. I can identify with that person wrestling to break free from an addiction. I'm all too familiar with the battle against enticing friends who seem to pull you ten feet backwards as you scratch and claw just to move an inch forward toward God. I'm aware of the overwhelming pressure from family members to succeed. But I also know of a God who desires to meet you right where you are, equipping you with every ounce of strength needed to resist and overcome! Give it all to Him. He will help you.

BROKEN BELIEVER

NAME: Paul

LOCATION: Acts 9

BROKEN VERSE: I have been crucified with Christ and I no longer live, but Christ lives in me. The life I now live in the body, I live by faith in the Son of god, who loved me and gave himself for me. (Galatians 2:20)

DESCRIPTION: When you think of someone in the Bible who was totally changed by the Gospel, Paul could not be any better of an example. Once a man who persecuted followers of Jesus (arresting, jailing, beating, and even killing them), he is encountered by Christ on the road to Damascus. This encounter completely changes his life. The spiritual scales are removed from his eyes, and he now sees Jesus in His glory and holiness. Paul soon becomes the most prolific spreader of the Gospel, traveling near and far to deliver this message of the Good News. He is the epitome of someone who endured the suicide process in order to fulfill a mission that was bigger than himself!

CHAPTER 5

DEAR COMPLACENT CHRISTIAN

"If you want to know how to backslide, the answer is leave off going forward and you will slide backward, cease going upward and you will go downward of necessity, for stand still you never can."

Charles Spurgeon

It was the summer of 2011, and I had just accepted an offer to be the Director of Basketball Operations at Stephen F. Austin State University. Life was about to change for me. I had recently graduated from college and was preparing to embark on a journey into coaching. It seems like I had only been home in Indiana for a few weeks after graduating, that I was packing my belongings once more and preparing to head down to Texas. I remember my mom trying to come up with alternatives to me driving down there. "Well you could always fly or take the bus…" she proposed. The problem was, the job required me to have some form of transportation while there. After much debate, she finally came to terms with the fact that I would have to drive. So she and my step-dad helped me buy a car – Happy graduation, Kyle. I was going to be making the 15-hour drive by myself. After loading up the car with my bags and hugging everyone goodbye, I hit the road to good ol' Nacogdoches, TX. I know, Naco-what!?!? Pronounced Nak-uh-doh-chiss, it's a small town that takes pride in considering itself to be "The Oldest Town in Texas." Now I'm not sure if you've ever driven long distance by yourself, but it can be pretty interesting to say the least. To this day, I'm not sure how I made that trip, twice. But I'll take the opportunity to explain what it was like.

As I began, I first had to navigate my way out of the city of Indianapolis. During this time, it required me to be alert and conscious of the turn-by-turn directions. Most of the city streets that I was traveling on were short distance and there were plenty of other cars around me, so I had to be engaged in the drive. Turn left here. Stop. Yield. Turn right up there. Merge. Slow down. The inner-city portion of the drive required me to be active, alert, and involved. I was conscious of everything that was going on around me. Many of us are when we drive. However, there was a point where I finally reached the highway. And as I traveled further and further, I approached the city limits and eventually hit nothing but open road. I'll now take this time to introduce you to a sweet feature of my car that I enjoy using in situations like this – cruise control. You're probably familiar with it, and most likely have used it as well. This system automatically controls the speed of the car, allowing you to relax. As the driver, you no longer have to concern yourself with pressing your foot on the gas pedal to maintain the speed of the vehicle. The cruise control system locks in your desired speed, and even allows you to accelerate and decelerate from controls on your steering wheel. It pretty much serves as an auto-pilot function. I no longer had to be as engaged in the drive. With no traffic lights, stop signs, or turns to make, I could freely enjoy this trip without any concern or worry. My alertness was replaced with a sense of tranquility and contentment.

This trip, beginning to end, is an exact depiction of what my spiritual life looked like at a point in time. It portrays the sense of comfort and half-heartedness I fell into in my relationship with God. The interesting thing is that this doesn't just describe me. It perfectly illustrates the state of contentment many people throughout the world are in; many who actually claim to follow Christ. It is the epitome of the comfortable Christian in today's society. The start of the trip I described captures the zeal and passion we tend to possess as followers of Jesus, often times when we first encounter Him. We're engaged in our purpose. We're aware of our surroundings, and alert to what God has called us to do in them. The Gospel sits in the driver's seat of our hearts, piloting every word, every thought, and every action. We're hungry for God. His will and desire are of such importance to us. As a result, worshipping Him is out of pure love, and serving others is fueled by intimate compassion.

Somewhere along the road of life, however, we encounter the open highway and hit that button that relaxes us into a state of comfort. We go into spiritual cruise control. This results in a contaminated mindset that infects the purity and passion of the heart. A sense of entitlement seeps in. Service becomes routine, and that zeal that once existed has diminished into mere indifference. Sometimes this state isn't something that someone "enters into." Rather, it can be what has always existed. It's what a person grew up in, and always has known. They've gone their whole life treating God this way, thinking it's ordinary, yet deceived by this normality. Regardless, it is a serious problem with which I'm all too familiar. I know because I experienced it firsthand. And now I'm currently witnessing it infiltrate our culture.

TO WHOM IT MAY CONCERN

This chapter specifically was birthed from intimate moments of quiet time with God. The goal here is to challenge and encourage you by expressing what God placed on my heart during those moments I spent with Him. The reason I prayed so much about this chapter is because I never intend to mislead. Nor do I aim to make anyone feel inadequate. This is easy to do when speaking from human perspective. However, I didn't want my thoughts and opinions to appear in any shape or form. Instead, I wanted the Holy Spirit to lead me on this topic. I wanted Him to elaborate on this issue that is deceiving people worldwide. I wanted His words to convict, yet comfort and inspire. During this time of prayer, a specific word was constantly whispered to me. This word encompasses the heart problem of people. It screams out the status of the church. And it perfectly labels the matter of self-righteousness that drives people into a deluded outlook on following Jesus. This word is **Complacency.** The more I pondered and mulled over that word, the more it made sense. Complacency, by definition, is a feeling of satisfaction with the way things are. It is approval of the status quo, often accompanied by an unawareness of danger or trouble. I subsequently decided to address "The Complacent Christian" through the sharing of my personal experiences. In doing so, it requires me confronting others in the same manner that I had to confront myself. I was forced to look in the mirror. Disgusted by the reflection of contentment and spiritual appeasement that stared back at me, I knew something had to change.

As you read this, I hope you receive it with an honest and open heart. Ultimately, I alone can do nothing. I have no power to change anyone, nor influence your thinking. And it's not my intention to do so. Only the Holy Spirit can contest and convict, as He leads you toward understanding and revelation. My prayer is that what you're about to read encourages you to ask God to show you yourself. More importantly, I pray it is followed by corrective action where applicable. This is a call to action.

DEAR COMPLACENT CHRISTIAN,

You are simply satisfied with being "good enough." You do just enough to consider yourself a Christian, and to appear good before others. You even do what Christians do to put up the image of a follower. This might include occasional prayer, morning devotionals, and a spiritual post on social media every now and then. You don't truly want to know Jesus and be completely changed by Him, just only looked at as "trying" to do better. You are content with barely sliding in the back door of heaven, just as long as you don't end up in hell. Unfortunately, many people who THINK they're on the heaven train will find out that they are mistaken. These are those who never truly sought Jesus. They went through the motions, prayed the prayer, and even maybe did the rituals. But when you talk about actually knowing Jesus, He couldn't be any more of a stranger. Jesus wants to actually know you! He does not just want the activities that seem to qualify people as Christians. He desires a full and intimate relationship, with a changed heart and a turning away from sin.

> *** *"Not everyone who says to me, 'Lord, Lord,' will enter the kingdom of heaven, but only the one who does the will of my Father who is in heaven. Many will say to me on that day, 'Lord, Lord, did we not prophesy in your name and in your name drive out demons and perform many miracles? Then I will tell them plainly,* **I never knew you.** *Away from me, you evildoers!'"* (Matthew 7:21-23)

Complacent Christian, you're okay with just partially following Jesus. You're content with halfhearted commitment, but refuse to dedicate your whole self to him. He has some of your life, but there are certain aspects of it that you refuse to surrender. You compartmentalize your life and select which parts of it you're willing to allow God to have:

"Jesus, I want You to be part of this relationship with my significant other, but don't ask me to give up pre-marital sex. That's too hard, I can't control my desires."

"If You could help me get this job, that would be great. But don't ask me to be a light for you in that environment. I don't want my co-workers thinking I'm weird by telling them about Jesus."

"Jesus, I'll give you some of my time, but don't ask for too much of my money. This is mine, and I worked hard for it."

*** *"In the same way, any of you who does not give up everything he has cannot be my disciple."* (Luke 14:33)

Complacent Christian, you measure yourself in comparison to the faults of other people. You qualify your goodness by quantifying your good works, and relating them to those of fellow believers or even unbelievers. You find the worst person you know, and use them to make yourself feel good because their sins are "more severe" than yours.

"As long as I'm not doing what He's doing, I'm ok. At least I'm not as bad as so and so."

Sin should never be compared. The primary reason your own sin doesn't bother you is because you view it in relation to others, instead of viewing it as it relates to God. The approach we should have is, "God help me to see sin the way You do." In addition, you fail to realize that the foot of the cross is level ground upon which we ALL stand. No one is more holy, no person is at all righteous, and no child of God is less loved!

*** *All have turned away, they have together become worthless; there is no one who does good, not even one.... For all have sinned and fall short of the glory of God.* (Romans 3:12, 23)

Complacent Christian, you are satisfied with merely going to church. In actuality, your church attendance is what generates your feeling of being a Christian. You routinely go to service, and sit in the same spot if possible. You become uncomfortable if service begins to run longer than normal because it's interfering with your day. You're content with a good message and lunch afterwards, followed by your regular Sunday nap. This leads to you mentally checking the box under the spiritual section of your weekly "To Do" list.

It isn't too much to say that this mentality transcends into your view and actions toward God. You treat Jesus the same way you treat your Sundays – on a schedule. Culture has trained your mind to place Jesus on a timetable that revolves around you. Jesus, however, asks us to give Him our whole selves, and not just part of our day.

Complacent Christian, you mistakenly use grace as an excuse to indulge in sin. You are somewhat familiar with the doctrine of grace, but have manipulated it to justify your immoral behavior. You frequently mistake God's grace for permission. You don't understand that grace does not excuse your pursuit of sin. It should actually involve comprehending that there is a consequence for it! That comprehension then should result in a passionate appreciation; a love for the Extender and His unmerited compassion; a love so deep that you no longer desire to pursue the sin that Jesus died to free you from. Truthfully, the grace of God does not say that it's okay to sin. It doesn't excuse it. And it certainly doesn't permit it. It pushes us away from it! It leads us toward holiness, and instills a desire within us to mirror Jesus. Furthermore, knowing that it is undeserved should only propel you to solely engage in activities and behavior that please Him. Read the following scripture. Pray over it. Read it again, and ask God to make known to you the biblical concept of grace. It will undoubtedly drive you to your knees.

> *** *"For the grace of God that brings salvation has appeared to all men. It teaches us to say "No" to ungodliness and worldly passions, and to live self-controlled, upright and godly lives in this present age,"* (Titus 2:11-12)

Complacent Christian, you are familiar with Christian culture, but have yet to encounter Jesus personally. You're well acquainted with church service, the building, and the activities that take place during service. You might even praise and worship, or serve in a particular ministry, but only out of habit because it is what "church people" do. Religion and routine have turned you into a robot. Instead of church being who you are, it has become where you're accustomed to going. You DO church. As a result, you've become immune to the transforming effects of the Gospel. You've become "familiar with God." And familiarity breeds insensitivity. Honestly, you're not alone. There are many people who culturally identify themselves as Christians, but biblically aren't followers of Jesus.

Complacent Christian, you don't truly desire to grow closer to God. You just want to remain at a proximate distance, so that you can still hold on to your life. You use the phrase, "God knows my heart" to validate your lack of commitment. This comforts you to continue in your sin, creating a false sense of security in your imperfections. You must realize, however, that the heart is innately perverse! Yes, God knows your heart. He knows that it is wicked. He knows that it is hardened, and that His grace won't be treasured until you ask Him to melt that ice-cold heart of yours. Listen, our actions and deeds are an expression of our heart. Everything we do flows from it. That's why God tells us to guard it! (Proverbs 4:23). The heart is only refined through constant communion with the Father. Instead of using His omniscience to justify our actions, we should perpetually seek His guidance of them. True Christianity derives from a yielded position of desiring to actually know God's heart, and disposing of the excuse that He knows yours!

> *** *The heart is deceitful above all things and beyond cure. Who can understand it? "I the Lord search the heart and examine the mind, to reward a man according to his conduct, according to what his deeds deserve."* (Jeremiah 17:9-10)

Complacent Christian, you blend in with the rest of the world. You look and act like those who don't know Jesus. Your language is no different. You desire and partake in the same things they do, creating no discrepancy amongst you. In a world where we have been called to be set apart, there really is no distinction about your character. You're content with fitting in with the rest of the culture and embracing the societal norms. Am I saying that you must dress in full clothing head to toe? No. Am I saying that you are to walk around with a bible everywhere you go, carrying a picket sign that says JESUS on it? Of course not. I'm simply advising that it is very possible to engage culture where it is, and still live radically for Jesus. To be clear, our faith is in no way defined by how we look or the amount of swear words that come out of our mouths. But it is expressed boldly from a strong desire to be holy as God is holy. That word holy is spiritually tied to a sense of consecration. God doesn't want you to feel miserably obligated to living this holy life. That never works. He wants to implant in you the mindset that this world is just temporary; that your true citizenship is in heaven. And that as believers, we have been called out of darkness and into a marvelous light!

*** *You adulterous people, don't you know that friendship with the world means hatred toward God? Anyone who chooses to be a friend of the world becomes an enemy of God.* (James 4:4)

Complacent Christian, you have an issue with talking about Jesus around other people, especially your peers. You fear that, in doing so, they will no longer want to engage with you. That you'll be considered a bible thumper. You're more concerned about appeasing them than leading them to salvation. Thus, you shrink back. You allow the opinions of others to deter you from effectively fulfilling the great commission given by Jesus to go and make disciples. Trust me, I get it. No one wants to be looked at as "weird." But it is spiritually hazardous to seek the approval of man above the approval of God. You have made an idol of their thoughts. It's foolish to allow others' opinions to dictate your level of passion for Jesus. No matter what, people should be able to see Christ in you. Not that we, as Christians, are perfect by any means. But our time spent becoming one with Him should naturally produce a Christ-likeness that illuminates any and all environments we encounter.

*** *"You are the salt of the earth. But if the salt loses its saltiness, how can it be made salty again? It is no longer good for anything, except to be thrown out and trampled by men. You are the light of the world. A city on a hill cannot be hidden. Neither do people light a lamp and put it under a bowl. Instead they put it on its stand, and it gives light to everyone in the house. In the same way, let your light shine before men, that they may see your good deeds and praise your Father in heaven."* (Matthew 5:13-16)

RELATIONSHIP OR...ROUTINE?

I remember sitting down eating lunch at work one day. I would always read while eating, and I happened to be studying a New Testament textbook at the time. Not too long into my reading, a co-worker whom I had developed a relationship with came into the room. He noticed I was reading, but wasn't sure what it was specifically. "Are you taking some kind of a class? Studying for a test?"

"No, just doing some general reading," I replied.

He kind of looked perplexed. "General reading? I guess that's cool. Do you read frequently?"

I told him that I haven't always enjoyed reading, but as of late its something that I took pleasure in. He asked what kind of books I usually read, and what I happened to be reading at the moment.

"Well, I'm actually going into ministry. So I'm doing some studying about the New Testament of the Bible."

His whole countenance changed. I wasn't sure if my answer caught him off guard, or if he just was uncomfortable. I've found that conversations regarding God have a funny way of evoking that kind of response. As we continued talking, he began confessing how he wished that he could go to church. He had to work on Sundays, and was unable to attend due to his schedule. I showed empathy, and identified with his struggle, having once been on a work shift that caused me to miss church myself for a while. I explained how important it was for me to find alternatives (like bible studies) and to be around other believers, despite my inability to make it to Sunday service. Subsequently, I mentioned to him that I led a men's bible study on Thursday evenings, and that I would be more than happy to have him join us if he was willing. I began telling him about the group and how it was like a brotherhood where men can open up about life, have genuine dialogue, and encourage one another. I saw the look on his face change again. "That's cool. But I usually like to spend time with my son when I'm not working so...I don't know. Sounds cool though." I could tell he was trying to politely object. It wasn't the first time I've experienced this kind of deflection from men. Heck, I used to do it. I was the king of excuses when it came to that stuff. I wanted absolutely nothing to do with anyone's invitations to bible study, church service, or anything that involved God. I was good in my own little world. After objecting, my co-worker went on to say, "I really just want to get back in my routine: having my weekends off, waking up Sunday morning, getting dressed, going to church, coming home to take a nap, and watching NFL football the rest of the day. That's what I miss."

I told him I understood and that the invitation was always there. He took my number and I encouraged him to contact me if he happened to become interested. But part of me was hurt. Not by him declining my invitation. I was hurt by the complacency that was vocalized as he depicted the true desires of his heart. It was exactly as he stated, "I just want to get back in my routine." Routine – something that is spiritually decapitating Christians everywhere. My co-worker wanted to return to his routine spiritual life, accompanied by additional Sunday entertainment. He didn't truly miss the opportunity to worship and commune with God, only the pre-game ritual of attending service before engaging in other customary Sunday occurrences.

From childhood, many Christians are exposed to this routineness. It is easy to create an atmosphere in the household of 'It's Sunday, we *have* to go to church again. Because its what we do here.' Soon, a routine mentality is developed, and a numbness to the Gospel seeps in. An increase in age doesn't remove the feeling of being dragged to church when no true understanding of Jesus exists. So although a person is old enough to no longer be dragged by their parents, it's still possible for them to be dragged by guilt. Allow me to clarify by saying that there is certainly nothing wrong taking our children to church. That isn't the point I'm making. The Bible instructs us to raise them in the Lord, and church is a vital part in this occurring. The problem arises when we don't emphasize to them the importance of developing a personal relationship with Jesus - the essentiality of knowing Him for themselves. This relationship is what ultimately transitions us as Christians from the mentality of "Its Sunday, I have to go to church" to "I *get* to go church!" It removes any sense of obligation, and replaces it with a privileged joy and a hunger for spiritual growth. This is eventually what exterminates the complacency that so many Christians suffer from as well. And for many of us, that genuine relationship is still something that has not been experienced.

But think about it. How often do we treat Jesus the same way my work associate described? We take our busy schedules, and squeeze Him in when it is convenient for us. We praise and worship, saying "Hallelujah" for a few hours prior to engaging in a plethora of other secular activities. That is the problem. We make Him only part of our schedules, when the reality is: He is not satisfied with partial attention. True submission occurs when you acknowledge that it's not God *plus* your agenda, but that He IS the agenda! He refuses to compete with your weekly itinerary, but instead desires that you replace it with Him! Everything we choose to do in life should surround God – every action, every decision, every thought, and every word. This is the true definition of the phrase "Jesus at the center of it all." When we take this approach, we no longer settle for complacent worship. Our service becomes fervent. And we are fueled and lead by a passionate fire that comes directly from Jesus Christ himself.

TEMPERATURE CHANGE

While we might not see anything wrong with our spiritual complacency, Jesus does. I'm reminded of a group of people in the Bible who possessed this same mindset. They likely exhibited many of the same behaviors previously described. Jesus directly confronts their unstable ways. In Revelation 3, Jesus speaks to the church in Laodicea regarding their halfhearted approach.

> *I know your deeds, that you are neither cold nor hot. I wish you were either one or the other! So, because you are lukewarm—neither hot nor cold—I am about to spit you out of my mouth.* (Revelation 3:15-16)

Lukewarm - Neither hot nor cold. What an accurate statement! I remember the time I first read that passage. I read it over and over again in disbelief. The feeling it gave me is indescribable; almost sickening. I honestly think I trembled just envisioning Jesus spitting people out of His mouth; People who spent their lives suffering from this severe disease of indifference. When looking at that word "spit", some translations actually use the words spew or vomit. Can you believe that? These words usually describe what happens when food is consumed, but cannot be stomached. As a result, it is regurgitated in disgust! Jesus says He will actually vomit them out of His mouth because He cannot stomach their complacency; their indifference is distasteful.

For me, what brought these feelings of discomfort was not picturing the people of Laodicea per se, but the fact that I saw my own self in that passage. I placed my feet directly in that scripture and imagined Jesus standing in front of me saying, "I know your deeds, Kyle. You are neither cold nor hot. I wish you would just choose a side!" Talk about gut-wrenching. I had to face myself. I had look at how I was living. I was treating God like an insurance policy; a 'Just in case' agreement. I didn't want to totally commit myself to Him because I still had some personal desires I wanted to pursue. I wanted to live with one foot in the world, and the other foot (more like just the tip of my toe, not my whole foot) on Jesus' side. And if anything happened, if I ever got in a bind, I wanted to be able to pull out my grace card to excuse my sin. Jesus doesn't want to be our 'Just in case.' He wants to be our One and only! But you must look at yourself and become uncomfortable with being comfortable. It is this honesty with ourselves that produces such a reverence for Jesus that we seek to use every part of our lives as an opportunity to serve Him. Such fear removes any sense of "somebody-ness" that you have about yourself, and moves you to surrender everything you are to the One who holds your very life in His hands.

Let me clarify something: There is absolutely nothing we can do to earn God's grace. It is completely unmerited and undeserved. It has been bestowed upon us as a gift, and it saves us through our faith (Ephesians 2:8). This was done nearly 2,000 years ago on a cross. So if you're taking this as a call to go out and perform moral deeds and act "good" in an attempt to be in right standing with God, then forget it! That's legalism. And that's exactly what shouldn't be done. We are not good enough to earn His grace, and we never will be. The Bible says our righteous acts are like filthy rags to God (Isaiah 64:6), so there is absolutely no way you can work your way into heaven. That is why the Gospel is so amazing. So, remove any thoughts of obtaining salvation through your works. God does not expect that. There is, however, a responsibility that comes with accepting Christ; A mandate given – to love. Love God with all your heart! You love God because He provided a way of escape from eternity in hell through Jesus. Such love inherently creates a willingness to love others and introduce them to the same type of relationship you have with Christ. It changes your thinking. It alters the way you perceive others. It modifies your behavior – the words you speak and actions you perform. It creates within you a desire to live holy, out of gratitude. It changes your life! This, my friend, is regeneration.

Ultimately, there comes a time when you're no longer satisfied with standing on the sidelines wearing the Christian jersey. You know that you have been called to get in the game. You recognize that Jesus does not desire for us to straddle the fence in comfort. Many of us think we're safe in this position, though. But Jesus warns us that we aren't! While it might seem easier to casually meander through this Christian life, God has called us to so much more. He wants you to break free from your complacency. He informs the church of Laodicea in that same passage, "I correct and discipline everyone I love. So be diligent and *TURN* from your indifference." (Revelation 3:19 NLT). He told them to turn from their indifference, which is a call to pure repentance. What does this look like? It means exactly what it says – to TURN! This involves having a change of heart about your sinful complacency. Jesus clearly states that He wishes we were either on one side or the other. You're either up or down, but Complacent Christian you must get off the middle of the teeter totter!

BROKEN BELIEVER

NAME: Nicodemus

LOCATION: John 3:1-21

BROKEN VERSE: "Rabbi, we know that you are a teacher who has come from God. For no one could perform the signs you are doing if God were not with him." (John 3:2)

DESCRIPTION: Nicodemus was a Pharisee. The Pharisees were a group of religious leaders who prided themselves on enforcing the Mosaic Law, traditions, and legalism. Sadly, many hypocritically lived against the very laws they imposed on others. But Nicodemus appears to be different. It becomes clear that Nicodemus is no longer content with his life of religious obligation. He recognizes Jesus Christ for who He is, and realizes that there has to be more to this life he's living. He truly wants to have a relationship with Jesus! So much that he approaches Jesus at night. Jesus has a serious conversation with Nicodemus, informing him of one critical component of being a follower – spiritual rebirth. "Very truly I tell you, no one can see the kingdom of God unless they are born again." (John 3:3). Ultimately, we see a follower who was not satisfied with spiritual complacency. He yearned for more, and did what was necessary to ensure he received it!

CHAPTER 6

YEAH, BUT...

"There are only two kinds of people in the end: those who say to God, "Thy will be done," and those to whom God says, in the end, "Thy will be done."

C.S. Lewis

There was a young man visiting my church once whom I had not seen before. While we have guests visit all the time, I could tell there was something different about him. Soon, I noticed that he was attending weekly. Sometimes he would even bring his friends with him. I thought this was admirable, because he surely didn't look like your average church goer. He'd appear often times in dress down attire, and sit in the back pew. I noticed that he was quite reserved, hardly speaking to anyone. So as one of the leaders of my church's Men's ministry, I made an effort to reach out to him one day after service. "Hey man, my name is Kyle. I've been noticing you here frequently. I just want to introduce myself and let you know that we have a men's ministry here that is pretty awesome, if you're interested." He thanked me, told me his name, and looked forward to receiving more information about the ministry. We exchanged numbers, and I assured him that I would be in touch.

One day after service I offered to meet with him outside of church to get to know him. He was very open to the idea. That week, we met up at a restaurant for lunch. I really didn't know what to expect, nor did I have any true plan going into the meeting. I just saw many similarities in him that I possessed at that age, and wanted to make myself available for any guidance he needed. As we sat down, we began to converse.

"So tell me about yourself. Where are you from?" I asked.

We talked about our backgrounds and what we do now. He was from Indianapolis like me. He recently dropped out of college and was back home working. After some time, I started asking him about church. "What brought you to our church?" I inquired.

"My mom started going there," he said. "She is the one who introduced me. After a while, she stopped attending. I figured I should just keep going." I decided to probe a little more to get an understanding of where he was in his walk with God.

"So do you like it? What do you think of church and how the word is presented?"

He told me he wasn't really sure what to think, and went on about his past experiences. "I've pretty much gone to church my whole life. My mom always made me go. Now, I come because I feel like it's what I'm supposed to do on Sundays. Half of the time I don't understand what the preacher is talking about."

I knew exactly where this conversation was going. I knew there was a reason I was drawn to him. I saw myself in him this whole time. Not that I grew up in church, but I could totally identify with feeling lost in church. It was time to start asking the more important questions. So I went a little deeper. "I understand," I responded. "Well let me ask you this: Who is Jesus to you?"

I could tell he had never really been asked that before. As we continued talking, he started opening up about a few things. "I mean, I believe in God. I know there is a higher power up there. But some things I still struggle with." I asked him to further explain.

"Well I want to follow Jesus, BUT…..I don't know. I guess I just struggle with some things. I still like to smoke weed. I do it a lot, almost every day. And I enjoy going out to the club on the weekends."

"I see. So you feel like if you totally commit to this Christian thing, you would have trouble giving up some things you like to do?"

"Exactly,' he said. "And my friends, those who I'm around a lot, they make it so hard to do what's right. I know it's not what I should be doing, but it's difficult."

I started sharing with him some of my similar past experiences – my love for the night life, and even my slightly-greater-than-normal obsession with alcohol in college. We talked for over an hour. I sensed that he appreciated how open I was regarding my past, and even some issues I still wrestle with today. It's always important to be transparent when sharing Christ with others. The worst thing that we can do in these situations is speak from our high horse. Our ability to open up and relate to them often helps to remove the barriers they've created when it comes to hearing truth. While I was careful not to affirm any of his behavior, I made sure he knew that he wasn't alone as he tussled with sin.

I wanted Him to also understand that being a Christian is not just about going to church. He somehow established this idea that church was where he had to go, whether it was out of guilt or obligation. I encouraged him to seek Jesus; to begin developing a relationship with Him. He is the only one who removes the scales from our eyes so that we can see. Too often, we tell a person to pray a prayer, ask Jesus to come into their heart, and that they're then saved – with no change of heart. And I didn't want to lie to this kid. Jesus said, "Whoever believes in me, as the Scripture has said, streams of living water will flow from within him" (John 7:38). By this He was referring to the Holy Spirit, Who is the power of our new lives. He begins and maintains in us a life-long process of change. We are baptized in the Spirit, Who works within us to help us become more like Jesus. This is what the kid was lacking, and it only comes from a broken heart that realizes that it needs a Savior. I didn't want to discourage him by making Christianity seem complex. However, I made it very clear to him that following Jesus is indeed costly.

Our conversation became very clear to me at a certain point. It was defined by one simple word; a conjunction that serves as the hinge in which fear, selfishness, and procrastination swing upon. The is word "BUT." This word is often used when people attempt to explain why completing an action is, or was, hindered. "I meant to call you like you asked, BUT something came up." Or "I want to help you out, BUT I'm kind of busy at the moment." Unfortunately, this same conjunction is used by individuals to rationalize why they're unable to submit themselves entirely to the authority of Jesus. And that's exactly what happened in our conversation. He stated, "I want to follow Jesus, BUT…" This is quite common. Busy schedules, sinful pleasures, and personal satisfaction can be the primary BUTS that cause us to justify our lack of submission. We allow our appetite for sin to take precedence over our appetite for holiness. Thankfully, we serve a faithful God. I'm so glad Jesus did not say "BUT" when it was time for Him to go the cross and die for us! "I mean, I would fulfill my mission to take away the eternal penalty of your sins, BUT you all are not worth it." Could you imagine that?

Truthfully, there is a multitude of people in the very same position of delay as the young man I spoke with. It might even be you. One of the greatest issues we face in deciding to follow Jesus is overcoming the fact that it requires sacrifice. It is a tough pill for many individuals to swallow. I know it was for me. This sacrifice was probably one of the biggest deterrents to me fully committing my life to God. Some of you can identify very closely with me. You begin to reason by saying, "I have my whole life ahead of me. Why should I give everything up now for that? Maybe I'll do it when I'm a little older." As we go a little further, we will dissect this disposition, looking at what Jesus has to say about the 'BUT mentality' that is spiritually damaging so many people.

RIGHT INTENTION, WRONG MENTALITY

As a high school and collegiate student-athlete, I remember constantly having to forgo a lot of things because of the schedule I had, and the commitment required to participate as a high-level athlete. In high school, while other students got to go home after school, I had to stay after for basketball practice. While my peers were able to stay out late on Friday nights, I had to be home at a reasonable hour because I had practice in the morning. Sometimes, this meant not going out at all. In college, while students were hanging out on campus and enjoying leisure time, my schedule consisted of study hall, mandatory team weight lifting, tutoring sessions, 3-hour practices, film sessions, and games; on top of going to class! As other students were at home with their families for Thanksgiving and Christmas break, we were in season and usually spent them at school or on the road, traveling. In no way am I discounting anyone else's efforts as a hard-working student. I'm quite aware of the time and effort it takes to be a college student alone. I'm only illustrating my experience. There was a price to be paid for the benefits that came with being a student-athlete. My college coach used to tell us, "You're giving us four years of your life, for a lifetime reward." This reward he spoke of was my full-ride athletic scholarship that allowed me to graduate with no student loans. At the end of the day, it required one thing – sacrifice.

When I first considered truly following Jesus, I took this same mentality into the relationship. It was based on me having to compromise, and I was not okay with that. Truthfully, it was quite discouraging. I would think to myself, "Man, this means I have to stop swearing. Does that mean I can't go to the club anymore? Hold on, that means I have to give up sex!" Certain habits and conducts began circling in my head. Needless to say, I had a problem with the idea of forfeiting parts of my life that I considered amusing. Therein lied a problem within itself. I was focusing the whole 'following Jesus' thing around me! It was all about what I wouldn't be able to do anymore, how I would no longer be able to talk, who I would no longer be able to hang around, and where I no longer would be able to go. I envisioned being a "true Christian" as living this unpleasant, boring, and dull life. My attention was primarily on everything that I would be losing, instead of everything I would gain! Honestly, I've found that so many people have the same contemplations when deciding to fully commit to Jesus. They count up all of the sinful pleasure that they'll have to give up in their life: the fun they'll miss out on, and the opportunities that will be lost. Sadly, it is a false reality.

Over time, I discovered that there was one critical component missing on my end of the deal – LOVE. I was trying to follow Jesus without understanding the basic principle to begin with! Love for the game of basketball is what pushed me through all of those moments in which I had to sacrifice in college. It motivated my actions, along with my commitment. Similarly, love is what inspires us as we commit our lives to Christ. You see, Jesus doesn't ask us to come after him with depressed hearts and regret. He wants us to affectionately pursue Him. He desires that you so intimately love Him and what He has done for you, that all of your pure motives and changed behavior are done with genuine love.

Where is this love found? It comes from understanding what Jesus did for you. It is discovered within the house walls of Caiphas, where the high priest gave Him an unfair trial late at night, accusing Him of blasphemy. It is found in the lashes upon His skin, as He was brutally flogged by the Roman soldier. It is found by hearing the people of Jerusalem scream at Pontius Pilate to "crucify Him!" We find our love for Jesus in the nails that were driven into His hands and feet on the cross, which shed His blood for our remission of sins. Finally, our love for Jesus is found in the empty tomb, as He was resurrected, conquering death and it's consequences! He willingly endured all of this…for you. True comprehension of His love for us creates an appreciative love for Him. It then produces an obedience that is no longer concerned with what you must give up. In comparison to what you're gaining (a lifetime reward of eternity in heaven) those things we must give up mean nothing!

YEAH BUT, IT'S COSTLY!

Jesus Himself often informed people about this love that is paramount in walking with Him. If we look throughout Scripture, there are several examples of people who wanted to follow Jesus, but on their own terms. But Jesus often had to inform them that there was a cost associated with their decision. He tested their love for Him, and their 'BUT mentality' proved to be evident in their hesitance. I'm reminded in Luke 9 how three individuals fit into this category. Jesus has just been rejected by the people of a Samaritan village. He is on His way to another village with His disciples, and is approached by the three individuals:

> As they were walking along the road, a man said to him, "I will follow you wherever you go." Jesus replied, "Foxes have holes and birds of the air have nests, but the Son of Man has no place to lay his head." He said to another man, "Follow me." But the man replied, "Lord, first let me go and bury my father." Jesus said to him, "Let the dead bury their own dead, but you go and proclaim the kingdom of God." Still another said, "I will follow you, Lord; but first let me go back and say good-by to my family." Jesus replied, "No one who puts his hand to the plow and looks back is fit for service in the kingdom of God." (Luke 9:57-62)

We must keep in mind that earlier in the same chapter (v. 23), Jesus clearly defined what it meant to follow Him. It was going to require suffering, discomfort, and maybe even death. Here, we first see a man who shows his zeal and willingness for Jesus, offering to follow Him anywhere. Jesus challenged His comfort by reminding Him that this walk does not involve penthouse suites and breakfast buffets. In reality, it wasn't so much about the actual place of rest. It was more so about, overall, being willing to sacrifice his sense of security. "Foxes have dens and birds have nests, but the Son of Man has no place to lay his head," Jesus replied. Translation: "You want to follow me? Cool. Well its going to cost you your sense of security – the safety you feel in your home, the coziness of your bed, the contentment of your familiar environments. How much do you love me now?" Question: Has your comfort limited your ability to follow Jesus? Jesus reminds us that walking with Him will cause us to reside in some unfamiliar territory.

He then asks another man to follow Him. We see this man's 'BUT mentality' clear as day. "Lord, first let me go and bury my father." Jesus' response is somewhat shocking. "Let the dead bury their own dead, but you go and proclaim the kingdom of God." Gosh! Let the dead bury their own dead? Imagine being told that after your parent has died. But Jesus isn't saying that family isn't important. He is actually comparing the love we should have for Him in relation to others – even our family. He goes even deeper in describing this comparison a few chapters later: "If anyone comes to me and does not hate his father and mother, his wife and children, his brothers and sisters--yes, even his own life--he cannot be my disciple." (Luke 14:26). I'll be honest in saying I didn't understand that verse for a while. You want me to hate my family? But I grew to understand that this isn't literal hate for our family members. It is an assessment of our love for Jesus. He is absolute, and every other relationship is relative; and not just family relationships. The man said, "First, let me go and bury my father." But what are you asking Jesus to allow you to do before coming to Him? "First, let me get out all of this pre-marital sex I want to have." "First, let me indulge in the night clubs and alcohol that I'm supposed to at this young age." This challenge is about attachment! Sadly, our attachment to family, friends, and worldly things can be a stumbling block in following Christ. But are you willing to follow Him, even if it means being disapproved by them? Christ is asking, "Am I really above all other things to you?"

Lastly, we see another individual who wants to take care of a personal matter before following Jesus. His request is to say goodbye to his family first. Jesus responds in a unique way. "No one who puts his hand to the plow and looks back is fit for service in the kingdom of God." Here, Jesus is addressing the person who feels the necessity to glance over his shoulder at what he will be missing. It is not necessarily about family, more so the person who could possibly second guess his decision. "Looking back" is often related to feelings of uncertainty. It is taking your focus off of the task at hand, and becoming concerned with what is behind you. Often times after I decided to follow Jesus, Satan would have me doubting that I made the right choice. "Look at what you will be missing out on!" I had to submerge myself in the comfort of God's promises, and remind myself of the destruction associated with my old life. Jesus reminds us that putting our hand to the plow (being his disciple and fulfilling His commission) requires an undivided heart. He knows indecisiveness can be a problem. He doesn't promise that the journey will be easy, but He does promise that it will be worth it. Don't let Satan or anyone else cause you to question your decision to follow Christ.

Jesus makes it abundantly clear that following Him is costly. He even encourages us to count the cost before making our decision (Luke 14:27-33). He wants you to be fully aware of what you're entering into. It is a relationship that could very well cost you your job, relationships with family members, even your life. Really ask yourself, "When is the last time following Jesus has actually cost me something?" When is the last time it cost you a friendship? When has it cost you a promotion at work? When is the last time it cost you your comfort? The primary reason following Jesus hasn't cost you anything is because your BUTs are greater than your belief. Your ideal form of following Jesus consists of staying at a far enough distance that allows you to sin comfortably, but relatively close enough to run to Him when you're in a bind; just nearby enough to approach and ask for a blessing, but not completely obey Him. I'm all too familiar with this type of trailing behind Jesus, because I did it. I wanted His blessings. But if I would have been asked to sacrifice something in my walk with Him, I would have said, "Kick rocks!"

He knows that many of us just desire the benefits of what He can do, rather than seeking to know who He actually is. What He actually wants, though, is your whole heart. He truly desires for you to discard your attachments that constantly have you saying, "Yeah, BUT..." Pray and ask God to give you an unrestricted desire for Him. Because it's an 'all or nothing' commitment.

YEAH BUT, MY FRIENDS...

During the conversation I had with the young man, he said something that resonated with me. It was an excuse that I was quite familiar with, because I too used it before. "My friends, they make it so hard to do what's right." I hear this frequently. So called friends who somehow determine our ability to obey the Lord. We want acceptance, so we mentally allow our friends to tether us to a life of sin. But allow me to explain something that is extremely important. The reason you continue partaking in this lifestyle is because you WANT to! Not because of your friends. No matter how much you look to blame your peers who continually entice you with negative influence and tempting environments, you still have a choice. And it is your flesh that leads you back to sin time and time again.

For me personally, I had to purpose my heart to place Jesus above the opinions of others, especially those I was following down a path of destruction. I had to make an eternal decision about what was more important. Often times, we fear that choosing to deviate from their negative influence will result in us being viewed as having a 'holier than thou' mindset. "Oh, you're too good to hang with us anymore? You're too holy to come out with us now? Let me guess, we're too sinful for you, huh?" (These are just personal remarks that I remember having to face at one time). Jokes and name-calling often serve as the substance of our friends' accusations. Truthfully, they are usually convicted by your decision to follow God, so they mask it with humorous reproach. But because we dread their criticism, we often relinquish our faith in order to soften their feelings of conviction. We give in to appease them, and return to the downward spiral of sin. Your friends' convictions from your obedience to Christ should never alter your commitment to Him. We are reminded by God several times throughout the Bible to not cling to the opinions and approval of others. It is amazing that He knows these very factors that impede on our desire to follow Him.

Am I now trying to win the approval of men, or of God? Or am I trying to please men? If I were still trying to please men, I would not be a servant of Christt. (Galatians 1:10)

Peter and the other apostles replied, "We must obey God rather than men!" (Acts 5:29)

Peer pressure is just another word for idolatry. It is simply when you have allowed your friends to become your god. Whether you care to admit it or not, your submission to their lifestyle is an attempt to gain and maintain their approval. You seek to be affirmed by them, and are afraid of what they will think of you if you choose to live right. It is these opinions that prevent so many people from wholeheartedly following Jesus. But you must remember, you will not stand before your friends on judgment day! No, you will stand before a holy and righteous God who will ask you why you sought their approval and not His. It isn't their validation that you will be seeking then. They won't be able to answer for you, nor will they be able to save you when it is time to give an account for your actions.

YEAH BUT, MY PAST...

One of the most common falsehoods that we tend to buy into is the lie of insufficiency; thinking our sin is too much for God to handle. It is a "Yeah, But" that sends us into hiding. We, as people, have an interesting way of limiting God's mercy in our own minds. We subconsciously allow Satan to trick us into putting a cap on the amount of grace God is able to distribute. I've met countless people who's 'BUT mentality' consists of untruthful thoughts of feeling inadequate and too far gone. Their approach is, "Yeah, But...I feel like I've done too much wrong in my past to come to Christ. It's too late." Perhaps you can associate with this. You think that you have to clean yourself up before coming into His presence. At that moment, you're declaring the blood of Jesus to be insufficient to cover, redeem, and empower you! Remember, He went to the cross with you in mind! And it is very difficult for you to receive the new life that He wants to give you if you are constantly dwelling on the mistakes of your old one!

I personally recall my own moments of feeling unworthy. I remember crying my eyes out one night, because I thought I could not break free from a sexual addiction. I felt so discouraged. Feelings of guilt became so heavy at times that I began to abandon any faith in the possibility of restoration. I'd tell myself that I was going to stop, but continuously found myself being pulled back in again and again. I would allow Satan to entertain my mind with deceptive feelings of hopelessness. He would whisper in my ear, "You keep returning to this same sin over and over again. Embrace it. God is tired of hearing your requests to be delivered. He's not going to forgive you." Lies. All lies. But it still caused me to hide in disgrace. Eventually I formed a sense of denial. I started to disguise my struggles and pretend that my infatuation with pornography didn't exist. This happens a lot to people. We question the possibility of forgiveness so much that we eventually attempt to hide our sin by sweeping it under the rug. It's dangerous to approach this area of life with an "Out of sight, out of mind" disposition. Know this: Sin is never removed by denying its existence! Opposing the truth does not change its validity. The Bible tells us that, *"Nothing in all creation is hidden from God's sight. Everything is uncovered and laid bare before the eyes of him to whom we must give account." (Hebrews 4:13)*

While we just saw how God sees all and knows all when it comes to our sin, I'm reminded of how the author of Hebrews also urges us to confidently approach God to receive forgiveness. *Let us then approach the throne of grace with confidence, so that we may receive mercy and find grace to help us in our time of need. (Hebrews 4:16)* Do you see that? He tells us to come to God's throne of grace with confidence! I know that may be somewhat difficult to grasp, but it is the truth. It doesn't instruct us to approach Him with timid spirits, apprehension, or doubt. Nor does it tell us to flee from His presence altogether, hiding in shame. Despite our sin, it is our assurance in God's compassionate promise of forgiveness that ushers us into His presence. He then enables us to overcome the strongholds that we feel ensnared by.

I soon found that the only answer to my running and denying ways was continual confession. That's where mercy resides. The walls of deception were finally knocked down when I discovered that the moment I commit the sin I perpetually commit, my first response should be to latch on to Christ! Instead of wallowing in our despair, we must stand – trusting in our Redeemer. Being broken is shadowed by our ability to assuredly run to the cross, pleading for help to turn from our sin and toward Jesus – every single time.

Listen, you are not too far gone. It is not too late. God wants to save you. The more you sulk in your misery of defeat, the more vulnerable you make yourself to the attacks of the Enemy. Repentance starts with confession, daily. It is time to stop playing the "God would never forgive me" card, and come boldly to the throne of our gracious Lord! Jesus is fully aware of the struggle you face in choosing to live right. He is mindful of the temptations you encounter on a daily basis. For He, Himself, was tempted.

> *For we do not have a high priest who is unable to sympathize with our weaknesses, but we have one who has been tempted in every way, just as we are — yet was without sin.* (Hebrews 4:15)

I love how that verse reassures us that Jesus can identify with our weaknesses. We often forget that He withstood vicious attacks from the devil also. Jesus, who came to earth fully God and fully human, is all too familiar with the enticing situations you're enduring. But He promises that on the other side of your obedience is something so much more rewarding! That is the beautiful thing about God. He allows us to make this choice. In no way does He need you, but He WANTS you. Can you fathom that? God, yes GOD, wants you! He's patient and faithful, even when we are not. Though you continuously turn your back to Him, He remains there willing to deposit His unreserved love into you. Despite all of your 'Yeah, BUT' excuses, He is still pursuing you. He's deeply desiring an intimate connection that will give you life. The moment you submit your heart to His, you will find that His comfort and peace are totally worth the sacrifice.

BROKEN BELIEVER

NAME: Unknown (Criminal On The Cross)

LOCATION: Luke 23:39-43

BROKEN VERSE: "We are punished justly, for we are getting what our deeds deserve. But this man has done nothing wrong." (Luke 23:41)

DESCRIPTION: Jesus was not alone when he was crucified on the cross. The Bible tells us that two other men – criminals – were crucified alongside of Him. One on his right, and the other on his left. Both of the Gospels according to Matthew and Mark express that these two men taunted Jesus, hurling insults at Him and mocking His deity. However, it appears that at some point, there was a change of the heart in one of these criminals. As one continued to mock Jesus – saying, "…Aren't you the Messiah? Save yourself and us!" (v. 39), the other began to truly see himself for the sinner that he was. He had a moment of brokenness, where He suddenly recognized the holiness of God! The broken criminal responds to his fellow criminal in rebuke. "Don't you fear God…. since you are under the same sentence?" (v. 40). A man who previously rejected Jesus as Messiah, was broken during the last hours of his life. His eyes were opened to Jesus' sinless life and sacrifice! "We are punished justly, for we are getting what our deeds deserve. But this man has done nothing wrong." He then asks with a contrite heart to be remembered by Jesus, who gives him the sobering words, "….Truly I tell you, today you will be with me in paradise." The criminal is wonderful proof that we are never too far gone to come to Jesus. If I had to guess, I'm sure he thought, "Yeah, But…" before asking Him for mercy. But his brokenness lead him to a place of humility, where he confidently received the grace of God.

CHAPTER 7

RELATIONSHIP GOALS

*"The Gospel does not call us to receive Christ as an addition to our life,
but as our life."*

- Paul Washer

Relationships – they are all around us, and its pretty hard to avoid them. We're involved in them with friends, co-workers, family members, and classmates. We develop connections with people throughout life that force us to interact and bond. For many of us, there even comes a time when we form a special relationship with someone on a deeper level than others. In our relationships with our significant others, we often aim to set goals – especially in America. The American Dream paints a fabricated picture that says fall in love, get married, be happy, buy a nice house with a white picket fence, have beautiful children, travel to exotic destinations, and live happily ever after. With this often comes the expectation of a perfect joyful marriage. But we're shocked when we notice that what we're involved in doesn't look like the American Dream we thought we signed up for. We've even come to the point of idolizing the perceived happiness of other couples (whether it be people we know or celebrities). We subconsciously wish that, for a moment, we could experience that same pleasurable lifestyle. We long for their life, their joy, and sometimes even their spouse. "Relationship Goals" is what we've come to label this fantasy, wishing that we can build our own little world of glee. But in reality, this isn't the truth. While marriage is a beautiful thing ordained by God, it takes work. It can be uncomfortable at times. Relationships in general require dual effort, and two people understanding the expectations of the relationship. If one person is not fully on board, then the relationship becomes a one-sided battle that lacks purpose.

One day, I was in the coffee shop doing some writing. I usually go there to release my thoughts. I actually don't go there for the coffee at all, because I've never been a big fan of coffee. I just enjoy the environment. There's a vibe of creativity that lingers in the atmosphere, and I like it. On this particular day, I happened to be sitting near a young teenage couple. There was a high school across the street from the coffee shop, and seeing that they had their backpacks with them, I imagined they walked over here together after school let out. As they were talking, I tried to tune them out. But my inquisitive ears couldn't help but overhear part of their conversation.

"We've been talking for a couple of months now," said the girl. "How do you feel about that? What are your thoughts about everything?"

The boy looked down at his cup of coffee as he replied, "I don't know. It's cool I guess."

"Cool? You guess? What does that even mean?" she exclaimed.

Still not making eye contact, he began to play with his coffee cup, circling the brim with his fingers. "Well, I don't know. I mean, I like hanging with you. You're pretty cool to be around."

"That's all?" she asked.

I could tell that this wasn't looking too good for my guy, who still couldn't bring himself to look up from his new found fascination with his coffee cup brim. She went on to express her feelings for him and how she was interested in taking the next step. But he appeared to remain hesitant, unsure, and unemotional. One thing was evident. He didn't feel the same way about her that she felt about him. At the root of it all, the girl was dying to know something. She yearned for an understanding that many women frequently seek in various stages of their relationships with men. She wanted to know one thing: "Where is this relationship going?"

While this might just be two kids with mixed emotions for one another, I strongly believe the principle is relevant in our relationship with Jesus. He often probes each and every one us, wanting you and me to ask ourselves that very same question: "Where is this relationship going?" It is a question that forces us to look at the true intentions of our hearts and assess our motives. Allow me to ask you something. What is your true motive behind your relationship with Christ? Have you ever asked yourself that question? If you're honest, you probably haven't. It's not something that many of us stop and think about.

What if every Christian's goal was to actually get to know Christ? I'm not talking about occasional conversations with Him, or showing up to church and singing to Him on Sunday mornings. If that was the case, everybody in the church would claim to know Him. No, what I mean is actually wanting to *know* Him. What if that was our one and only desire? Take away all of the religious customs and monotonous practices that tend to pollute our views of what it means to be a Christian. For a second, conceive in your mind the reality of having a pure relationship with the God of this universe; one that consists of unconditional love! Can you picture that? What would it look like?

GOAL #1: SUFFERING

Let's pretend someone walked up to you and asked, "Hey, do you know Michael Jordan?" First of all, you would probably be thrown off by their randomness. But once you got past it, I'm willing to bet that you would most likely respond to their question with a clarifying question of your own. It would probably go something like this, "You mean, do I know *OF* him, like have I heard of him? Or do I actually know him personally?" The difference between these two questions is quite significant. Wouldn't you say? There is a major difference between actually knowing someone and knowing of someone. Actually knowing someone implies that you have developed a relationship with them through meeting and spending time with them. On the contrary, knowing of someone infers that you are only aware of who they are. Just about all of us are aware of who Michael Jordan is, arguably the best basketball player to walk the face of this earth. But I'm willing to bet that you haven't developed a relationship with him by spending time in his presence. So none of us really know Michael Jordan.

Would you believe me if I said there are some Christians who only know *of* Jesus? As hard as it may seem to believe, it is the truth. Some people don't see anything wrong with this. Others might be deceived in thinking they actually know Him, but show that they only know of Him. I must express how dangerous it is to be content with this type of mindfulness.

The danger lies in the verity that sheer awareness doesn't get us into heaven. The Bible confirms that even the demons of this earth know who Jesus is! In Matthew Chapter 8, Jesus has just come off of a boat with His disciples and encounters two men that are possessed by demons. Upon His arrival, we see their admission of His Lordship:

> *When he arrived at the other side in the region of the Gadarenes, two demon-possessed men coming from the tombs met Him. They were so violent that no one could pass that way. "What do you want with us, Son of God?" they shouted. "Have you come here to torture us before the appointed time?"* (Matthew 8:28-29)

Now, one might argue that these were the men themselves talking to Jesus, and not the demons. But it only takes us to glance two verses further (v.31) to see that this isn't so: *The demons begged Jesus, "If you drive us out, send us into the herd of pigs."*

It is clear that the demons were speaking through the men, and that even Satan's associates believe who He is. They clearly acknowledge His existence and deity. Furthermore, James 2:19 says, *"You believe that there is one God. Good! Even the demons believe that – and shudder."* This eliminates any sufficiency in merely believing in God. So I must ask you a personal question: What differentiates you from the demons? What separates your belief from their form of belief?

The difference must rest in the intimate relationship that is developed through continuous time spent communing with Him. It is recognizing who you are as a sinner, acknowledging your need for a Savior, and desiring to grow closer to Him by any means necessary. In doing so, you are molded into His image, becoming more and more like Him daily. The difference is in your hunger for His glory to be illuminated in your life, so that others may see Him through you. And finally the difference is in your willingness to endure anything and everything to ensure that His name is proclaimed to others, so that they too may develop a loving relationship with the only Person who can give them eternal life. So, what separates our belief in Jesus from the demons'? It is our desire to know Him so closely, that He changes everything about us!

You see, it's easy to become familiar with religion. For many people, it's all they have experienced their whole lives. We can easily get caught up in empty traditions, routine services, and false ideologies. However, this isn't what our Lord has called us to. He desires so much more from us. More than anything, He wants us to actually know Him. And this should be our single greatest desire. Even as churchgoers and servants, it is possible to mistake familiarity with religion for knowing Jesus. Our acts of service, our biblical knowledge, and our roles within the church can easily cloud our heart's desire to truly know Christ. Your title or position in the church, in no way, means that you know Him. Sadly, many of us qualify our "knowing Jesus" by the deeds we have done, titles we have earned, and the amount of times we shout in church. It only takes for us to once again look at Paul as he explains what it means to know Christ. And it isn't in his titles or achievements:

...If anyone else thinks he has reasons to put confidence in the flesh, I have more: circumcised on the eighth day, of the people of Israel, of the tribe of Benjamin, a Hebrew of Hebrews; in regard to the law, a Pharisee; as for zeal, persecuting the church; as for legalistic righteousness, faultless.

*But whatever was to my profit I now consider loss for the sake of Christ. What is more, **I consider everything a loss because of the surpassing greatness of knowing Christ Jesus my Lord, for whose sake I have lost all things.** I consider them rubbish, that I may gain Christ and be found in him, not having a righteousness of my own that comes from the law, but that which is through faith in Christ—the righteousness that comes from God and is by faith.*

I want to know Christ and the power of his resurrection, and the fellowship of sharing in his sufferings, becoming like him in his death, *(*Philippians 3:4-10*)*

If you know anything about Paul, you know that he was one of the most religious men during the time of the start of the church. Formerly known as Saul, he was a Pharisee who demanded strict obedience to the Mosaic Law, and was so zealous for God that he began persecuting the Jews who were preaching about Jesus and the new covenant. Saul then has an encounter with Jesus who completely transforms his life. But as Paul is writing to the people of Philippi, he defines what it means to really know Christ. If we go back and read that passage, Paul is pretty much saying, "Look at my credentials. If anyone has a reason to be considered good enough in the flesh, if anyone should be able to settle for the status quo, if anyone could be considered knowledgeable…it should be me!" But he goes on to say about his accolades in verse 8, "...*I consider them rubbish, that I may gain Christ.*" That word rubbish used here in the Greek is *skybala*. It is translated in other versions as garbage or dung. Paul is comparing his former religious qualifications to rubbish in relation to actually knowing Christ! How much more should we? So what does it mean to actually know Christ then? You might have been asking that this whole time. Paul goes on to say in verse 10 that he wants "...to know the power of His resurrection and the fellowship of sharing in his sufferings, becoming like him in his death."

Sharing in his sufferings? The NLT says, "I want to suffer with Him, sharing in His death." As Christians, we have been called to share the Gospel. We have been called to stand out from a world that does not want to accept this truth. Our culture does not have a favorable view of us as Christians. As followers, we believe in things that clash with society. In saying this, it is not farfetched to say that knowing Jesus actually equates to suffering with Him. As we previously discussed, following Him is costly. And just as Jesus suffered - being rejected, talked about, and mistreated - we have similarly been called to suffer!

Can you truly say like Paul that you want to know Christ to the point of sharing in His sufferings? Here is the better question: When is the last time you suffered for the sake of the Gospel? Our relationship with Jesus is one that transforms us into His likeness, and with that likeness comes modern forms of persecution. Whether it comes from people at our job, our peers, or our family members, knowing Jesus should result in suffering. This might not sound appeasing, but the Christian life is not marked by comfort and security. In actuality, we should rejoice whenever we are persecuted. As Peter reminds us, *"But rejoice that you participate in the sufferings of Christ, so that you may be overjoyed when his glory is revealed. (1 Peter 4:13).* Timothy is told, *"In fact, everyone who wants to live a godly life in Christ Jesus will be persecuted,"* *(2 Timothy 3:12).* One thing is apparent: **knowing is suffering**, and it validates those of us who are in Christ Jesus. So I must ask you: Is your relationship goal to suffer?

GOAL #2: INTERRUPTION

For a majority of our relationship prior to marriage, my wife and I courted long distance. She was at Indiana University, and I was in

Washington, D.C. attending Howard University. Hundreds of miles separated us for several years. I would be lying if I said that it was easy. There were many road bumps along the way that forced us to totally rely on God for strength and reassurance. But I knew that if we could endure it, then we could make it through almost anything. During this distanced courtship, we had to be intentional about finding ways to communicate. We didn't have the luxury of just physically being in each other's presence sometimes, and enjoying one another's company. But eventually, it was something that we learned to cope with. We actually grew accustomed to this type of life after so many years of it; so much that it almost seemed normal. We tried to occasionally talk during the day, but our schedules often conflicted. So text message conversations usually sufficed, and phone conversations typically took place before turning in for bed. Some nights, we didn't talk at all. It was pretty routine at times, but we became used to it. We were content with being together, while physically being apart.

While our long distance relationship was by choice, I'm curious to know how many of us, as Christians, are subconsciously in this same type of relationship with Jesus. How many of us have become satisfied with Jesus not totally being in our lives, and just keeping Him some distance away to talk to on occasion? How relaxed have we become in being spiritually detached? The unfortunate truth about this type of "relationship" with Jesus is that it isn't biblical. Everything I see in the Gospels reveals how Jesus encountered people and completely interrupted their ordinary, routine lives.

After courting long distance, I moved back home to Indiana and proposed. One thing that we would always discuss is how different our lives were going to be once we got married. And boy was it different! One of the biggest changes that occurred was cohabitating after marriage. We previously spent so much time apart in our courtship, we actually had to learn to live together. Everything from cleaning habits to sleeping in the same bed became an issue. We were forced to deal with changes that we hadn't experienced before. One thing was certain, marriage interrupted our lives. If not hers, it certainly interrupted mine! My normal practices were quickly addressed and reformed. I could no longer live life in my "single" mind frame– leaving the toilet the seat up, drinking out of juice cartons, and spending money at my leisure. Marriage absolutely wrecked my traditional way of living, and I had to learn to be okay with that.

I submit to you that our relationship with Jesus should at some point consist of this exact type of change – interruption. Similar to how two people are joined together in marriage, knowing Jesus also symbolizes a joining together. It is becoming one with Him. And that oneness is accompanied by conviction and rebirth. Following Jesus is a commitment that results in Him "moving in" to your heart. It is a relationship that requires Him to shape, alter, and modify your normal practices – bad habits and all. Essentially, we must allow Jesus to interrupt our life! Many people want Jesus to be part of their lives, but don't want Him to interfere with certain parts of it. As a result, they attempt to negotiate the stipulations of the relationship with Him. "Look, I have a pretty good thing going right now. I do what I want, say what I want, and I go where I please. Don't come in here and start messing stuff up!" Imagine if I had said that to my wife upon moving in together. I would be single again in a heartbeat. But sadly, we often treat Jesus this way. We claim to believe in Him without embracing the behavior modification required to validate our true belief. And this cannot happen. Part of being broken is permitting the Holy Spirit to perform a heart transplant, substituting your old habits for those of a new person who is united with Christ.

> You were taught, with regard to your former way of life, to put off your old self, which is being corrupted by its deceitful desires; to be made new in the attitude of your minds; and to put on the new self, created to be like God in true righteousness and holiness. (Ephesians 4:22-24)

Our oneness with Christ is actually proven by a visible changed life. And truthfully, if your faith hasn't changed you, it hasn't saved you. We all must ask ourselves, "Does my life give evidence of a true Christian? Is the way that I'm living congruent with what I profess?" There came a point in my own life that I had to look in the mirror and ask myself those questions. And I didn't like the answer that I was forced to admit. I hadn't totally embrace Jesus in my life, I merely tolerated Him. I feared the interruption that came with allowing Him to move in. So instead of inviting Him in the house (my heart), I kept Him outside in the front yard. I knew that as long as He wasn't inside, I wouldn't have to deal with Him telling me to tidy up. I attempted to keep the door locked and blinds closed, so that I could live in my filth. This is not true relationship. I realized that Jesus wants full access to interrupt – house key, garage code, and spare key. Likewise, the Gospel must permeate your heart, completely renovating your behavior, your thinking, your life.

GOAL #3: GOD'S HEART

An essential goal of our relationship with Jesus should be to break us of any attempts to make the relationship about us. Today's Christian culture is infested with false doctrine that promotes this idea that God can give you whatever you want, as long as you believe. Materialism and selfish gain serve as the roots of the blessing tree in the American church. While Jesus contrarily told a rich man to sell all of his possessions and give to the poor if he wanted to truly follow Him (Matthew 19:21). He told another man in Luke 12 that "a man's life does not consist in the abundance of possessions…" (v. 15). But we somehow have allowed greed to propel our prayers and praises. Even if it's not seen as greed, the surrounding figure in many of our spiritual relationships is our own selves. Frankly, the main prayer needed to be prayed today is for assistance in emptying ourselves of ourselves.

Question: Do you truly want God, or do you only want the type of life you believe God can give you? Are you seeking His heart or are you seeking His hand? Our prayers must not consist of "bless me" requests that surround ourselves. Instead, they should be filled with intercessory for others and a desire to serve the Lord in the greatest capacity possible.

Often times, we treat God like some sort of spiritual ATM that we can approach for selfish withdrawals. Christian culture has reduced God to a personal genie, Whom we seek to appear at our beck and call. We go to Him requesting blessings upon OUR plans, healing for OUR family, and success in OUR life goals. But is He enough to worship alone? Would you claim that He is number one in your life if you weren't counting on Him to bless your endeavors? If you weren't trusting Him to help you attain that position you're working so hard for?

Don't confuse what I'm saying. Jesus is indeed a healer and a provider. He willingly spent a majority of his ministry helping the blind see, allowing the lame to walk, and even raising the dead! God provides as He sees fit. His power is sufficient, and in no way is He unapproachable for us. So I'm not discounting that truth. In fact, he expects us to draw near to Him seeking comfort and strength. The problem, however, lies in our man-made philosophies, where 'Name it and claim it' messages dilute the purity of the Gospel and fuel our egocentric hearts. The danger in this is that much of your supplication is outside of God's will. It's not biblical. Approaching the Lord with a personal laundry list often indicates that your motives are impure, and further reveals your wishes that are a result of self-centeredness. This transports us back to revealing what our true motives are.

We see an example of someone who had impure motives In Acts chapter 8, through a man named Simon. During this time, the church was in full force. Jesus had already ascended into heaven, his followers were being persecuted by radical Jews and religious leaders, and the church was being pushed beyond Jerusalem to fulfill the commission given by Jesus to preach the Gospel to all nations. In Samaria, a man named Philip was preaching the Gospel and performing miracles, converting many of the people into believers. In the town of Samaria was a magician named Simon. Prior to Philip's arrival, Simon took pride in being responsible for wowing these people with his wonders. The Bible says he "…practiced sorcery in the city and amazed all the people of Samaria…" (Acts 8:9). But once Philip arrived, everyone's attention was turned from Simon to Philip, and many were baptized, even Simon himself. *"Simon himself believed and was baptized. And he followed Philip everywhere, astonished by the great signs and miracles he saw."* *(v. 13).* On the surface, it would appear that Simon's faith was genuine. He gets baptized, and even starts following Philip. But it doesn't take long before we see his intentions revealed. Word gets back to the apostles regarding all that is taking place in Samaria, and Peter and John are sent there to pray that they receive the Holy Spirit. Upon them laying hands on the people of Samaria, the Holy Spirit is received and Simon is in awe of what He sees; so much that he attempts to buy this ability.

> *When Simon saw that the Spirit was given at the laying on of the apostles' hands, he offered them money and said, "Give me also this ability so that everyone on whom I lay my hands may receive the Holy Spirit."* *(Acts 8:18-19)*

Here we witness the true nature of Simon's heart. Outwardly, he was following the Christian crowd and even going through the rituals, but inwardly we see that his motive encircled his selfish desire for personal gain. He appeared to have a hidden agenda, not truly wanting God's heart, instead wanting God's gift. At the core, it was all about Simon, and what the Holy Spirit could do for him. Even after Peter rebukes him for his false belief, Simon doesn't express true repentance with a heart that desires to rightly understand what it means to know God. His sorrow is centered around the potential consequences of his actions.

There have honestly been times where I have found myself in Simon's shoes —seeking God's favor for personal reasons. Through intense prayer, I've had to ask God to remove any selfish intentions that reside in me, as all I want in this relationship is to serve Him with obedience. "God, I don't want to make this relationship about me. It's not about receiving my breakthrough. It's not about what miracles can be done in my life. Nor is it about acquiring my blessing. Instead, help me to fall so deeply in love with You that I'm able to BE a blessing to others! God, help me to not give with expectations of receiving. Allow me instead to give with assurance, knowing that if I never receive a single thing in this life, the fact that you saved me from a burning hell is good enough! God, help to understand that you owe me nothing!"

I often ask God to help me not be like Simon the magician. I want to live out the true ministry of the Christian life. Unfortunately, there is a hidden "give me" spirit that is deeply nested in all of us. We must constantly pray for the Holy Spirit to give us the power to bring it under subjection, and align our motives with God's will. When we are willing to seek His heart with no intentions of personal gain, it is at that point that God rewards us openly. The person who takes this Christian life seriously discovers freedom from being centered in themselves.

BROKEN BELIEVER

NAME: Peter

LOCATION: Matthew 26:69-75; John 21:15-23

BROKEN VERSE: …And he went outside and wept bitterly. (Matthew 26:75)

DESCRIPTION: Have you ever had a close relationship with someone? Have you ever been so close that you never wanted anything to happen to them? What if in a moment when they're being persecuted, you completely deny any affiliation with or knowledge of that person? Shady, right? Well this is exactly what happens with a man named Peter. Throughout the Gospels we see how Peter develops this intimate relationship with Jesus, becoming one of His inner circle disciples. He gains Jesus' trust to lead and carry forth the mission of the church in His absence. But in a moment where it appears Jesus could use Peter most (not that Jesus actually needed help), Peter abandons Him. After Jesus has been physically and verbally persecuted by the Sanhedrin, Peter completely denies Him and flees in terror. He then realizes what he has done and expresses a Godly sorrow that breaks him to the core. His repentant heart fills him with such guilt and shame for denying the One who he once was so close with! He probably thought Jesus was saying, "I thought you knew me? Now what's going on? Where is this relationship going?" Many of us can relate. When it seems like we've distanced ourselves from Jesus, it's easy to feel disqualified and disloyal. But what we see is that Jesus says none of those things when He sees Peter again. Jesus shines His grace upon Peter, letting him know that the relationship was never broken. He uses him to spear the launch of the church with the same faith and trust as before! God wants the same with us. Despite how badly you may think the relationship is too bad for repair, Jesus wants to remind you that He's still there. He still wants to use you!

CHAPTER 8

SEEING ETERNITY

"Five minutes inside eternity and we will wish that we had sacrificed more, wept more, grieved more, loved and prayed more, and given more."

Leonard Ravenhill

I wish this last chapter was easy for me. I wish it could just be smooth sailing going into the finish line. No, this is probably going to be the most difficult. Not difficult out of fear, but challenging in regards to authentically expressing this topic without compromising. It is imperative that it is presented in the purest manner, with no restrictions; No sugar-coated fluff to make it more appeasing or easy to take in; And no half-truths to satisfy the ear that wishes to be tickled. That should not, and must not, be done here. It's already done regularly by preachers all throughout America, who water down the message of the Gospel out of fear of disturbing the spiritual comfort of their members. As for me, I refuse to dilute something that requires total truth. And it is something that we can't afford to be wrong about. This isn't something to be taken lightly, or toss subjective views around with hopes that it's correct. I understand that, which is why I spent more time praying about this chapter than I actually did writing it. In light of that, it goes without saying that this is also the most important chapter. Why? Because one hundred years from now the only thing that will matter is how seriously you took this subject. It determines how you choose to spend this life, as well as the next one. They have a direct correlation. Sadly, there will be no do-overs, no re-do's, or second chances. My prayer is that if nothing else in this book captured your attention, you ask God for this chapter to be meaningful to you. I beg you, take to heart what I will brokenly be expressing here. This is not the most popular thing to discuss. Trust me, if I could get away with avoiding it, I would. But it is most necessary. We are talking about eternity.

HUSH, DON'T SAY THAT!

For the longest part of my life, I tried to avoid thinking about life after death, partly because I was ignorant about it. I deliberately refrained from engaging in conversations regarding eternity. When I did read the Bible, I skipped over parts that discussed God's wrathful judgment. One time in high school, I excused myself from a church service in which the sermon was about hell. I pretended that I had to go to the bathroom so I wouldn't have to sit and deal with any feelings of conviction or condemnation. Eventually, this evolved into me questioning hell altogether. Do people actually go to hell at all? I mean, everyone going to heaven isn't such a bad idea, right? How I wish this was true. I'd love to believe that no matter what we do, say, or believe in, there is a spot in heaven that awaits everyone on this earth. Sadly, many universalists believe this to be true. But in actuality, it is not biblical.

That view didn't last long for me. It became hard for me to believe that evil people should be permitted to go to heaven. Like many today, I soon began envisioning hell as a place reserved only for those who commit cruel and heinous acts, like mass murder, rape, harming children, etc. I threw atheists in that category as well, figuring someone who doesn't believe in God at all shouldn't be allowed in to His heavenly gates. In my mind, these types of people actually deserved to be punished. Crazy, right?

Looking back, I see that this view of hell was only an attempt to assure myself that I was a "good" person. Although I hadn't fully committed to following Jesus, I thought to myself, "God wouldn't punish someone like me. I treat people decently and I have a good heart. I might not know a lot about Him, but I at least attend church occasionally and pray every once in a while. That's good enough, right?" I thought being kind and generous was sufficient to at least get me in the back door of heaven. My attitude was, "I might not be in the VIP line, but I'll manage to get in there somehow. I'm not the best person, but I'm fairly good." Once again, a totally false view. But I figured that my good manners and decent acts put me in a better position than some. This actually was me masking my true uncertainty about my future. Instead of confronting it, I intentionally dodged the notion of me possibly ending up in a place of eternal torment. I used my own rationale to assemble my own truth about something our Almighty God established. Have you done this? Have you purposely ignored the fact that you will end up in one of two places after you die? Or have you even disposed the impression altogether that a loving God would send people to hell? This is even more dangerous. Evangelical preacher, J.C. Ryle advised, "Beware of manufacturing a God of your own: a God who is all mercy, but not just; a God who is all love, but not holy; a God who has a heaven for everybody, but a hell for none!" I know, it's a lot easier not to think about it. But this isn't something that we can just place on the backburner to address once we muster up enough courage to overcome our fear and doubt. Nor is it something you ought to play Russian roulette with, living with a 'Whatever happens, happens' mindset.

Yes, that is exactly what Satan wants though. He takes joy in the fact that people feel that hell is too sensitive of a subject to discuss or even think about. He doesn't even want me mentioning it to you right now. His popular sales pitch is, "It is too offensive. Don't talk about it. Don't preach it. Don't even think about it." I'm not saying that we should spend our time feeling condemned. But it does require acknowledgement and awareness. Satan knows that the longer he can distract people into discarding hell's existence, the more souls he can potentially have join him there when he is sent (Revelation 20:10-15). Furthermore, even if you do believe it exists, he purposefully seeks to persuade you that good people wouldn't possibly go there. It comes from his same tactful beliefs used to deceive Eve into partaking of that forbidden fruit, "You will not surely die" (Genesis 3:4). It is his conniving spirit that lures the mind into denial and misguidance of what our salvation is based on. But if this is truly the case, wouldn't you want someone to warn you about such deception and lies?

I'm here to tell you that our salvation, in no way, is based on being good. I want you to visualize something. Imagine standing before our Lord and Him asking you, "Why should I let you into heaven?" What would you say? Have you thought about that? Would you say, "Well Lord, I was a good person."? The unfortunate thing is, good is a relative term by human standards. What is considered good to one person isn't always the same to someone else. Ask pretty much anyone if they consider themselves to be a good person, and nine out of ten will probably tell you, "Yes." Maybe even all ten will. Just about every funeral we attend has an atmosphere filled with conversations of someone being a good person. We regularly define the term "good" by our own standards.

Here is the scary truth. No one is good! The Bible tells us, *"...There is no one righteous, not even one;" (Romans 3:10)*. Every last one of us have sinned, and we all fall short of the glory of God (Romans 3:23). So, the only way to measure your so-called "goodness" then is by God's standards – His perfect law. You would have to keep this law your whole life, without fault! And seeing that all of us have told a lie (some of us today alone) amongst a number of other sins, I submit to you that you have not and cannot keep His perfect law. I'm sorry to break the bad news, but you are not a "good person." And neither am I. You can be as kind as you want, doing as many good deeds possible, and still perish. You are not good enough and you never will be. Because we don't measure up to God's standards, we are deserving of his holy wrath - punishment in hell. But do you want to know something? God saw someone who IS good! His name is Jesus. And since God still had to administer His wrath somehow, the only satisfaction that would reconcile man to Himself would then have to be made by God. He was loving enough to sacrifice His only begotten Son to do so. Jesus came to earth, lived a sinless life, and willingly went to the cross to substitute His righteousness for our unrighteousness. He satisfied the wrath of God, taking it upon Himself! And it is ONLY by believing in Jesus that a person is saved (Acts 4:12), no matter what deceptive lies the devil feeds you.

FIREFIGHTER

Knowing the good news that we just discussed, you would think that it would be communicated with as many people possible. But as previously mentioned, the common practice in culture today is to keep silent regarding this matter of eternity. Many Christians are comfortable only worrying about their own salvation. We have strapped on our pew seatbelts, and are waiting for Jesus to come back. "Don't ask me to share the Gospel, I have my own problems to worry about." This is certainly not the mentality that the Bible promotes. In fact, it tells us to do the exact opposite. Jesus actually instructs us to proclaim from the rooftops what

He has whispered (Matthew 10:27). Imagine if we all took this approach, telling everyone who was willing to listen about the Good News? If hell is really a place of fiery torment, our brokenness should likewise produce an unquenchable desire to rescue others from the flames while there is still time! In the Bible, Jude commands us to do just that!

> *"Keep yourselves in God's love as you wait for the mercy of our Lord Jesus Christ to bring you to eternal life. Be merciful to those who doubt; snatch others from the fire and save them;..."* (Jude 1:21-23)

Picture this: You come home one day and see that your neighbor's house is on fire, but they don't know it. You see them through the windows just carrying along inside – laughing, eating, and dancing. They're totally unaware that their lives are in danger. You notice mounds of flames and smoke being exuded from the roof. At any moment, it could collapse. At any moment, they could be consumed by the flames or die from smoke inhalation. What would you do? Would you casually walk across the yard and whisper in a moderate tone, "Excuse me, are you aware that something over here is burning? You might want to check it out." Would you ignore it altogether, hoping that they eventually come to realize that their home is engulfed in flames? Or would you run over there as fast as you could, banging on the door, jumping up and down, screaming at the top of your lungs, "HEY! YOUR HOUSE IS ON FIRE! GET OUT! GET OUT! GET OUT!" I would presume that you would do the latter, screaming with everything in you to save them. At least, I hope you would.

Likewise, this is me screaming with everything in me that eternity is real! Hell is real! Eternal fire is real! And it isn't just for atheists and people who commit extremely heinous crimes. It is reserved for anyone who hasn't accepted the Gospel, confessing Jesus as their Savior, and truly making Him Lord of their lives – placing their names in the Book of Life (Revelation 20:15). And if you know this, then you should be screaming the same thing to others. It breaks my heart because I look around and see so many people oblivious to it. They're carrying on like the neighbors in the house - eating, drinking, and being merry. They live with total disregard for where they will spend the millions upon millions of years after they are taken from this earth. Many have absolutely no idea! While others simply don't care. Regardless, some place dangerous awaits them and I would be heartless if I didn't stress the severity of it. So, I must ask you: **If you died tonight, are absolutely sure that you would go to heaven?**

If your answer was No, then that is a frightening thing. But the beautiful part of it is that it's not too late to change that uncertainty. I believe the most aggravating thought of many people who end up in hell will be knowing that they had an opportunity to avoid going there in the first place. How dreadful would that be? Knowing that your suffering could have been prevented. Now, this isn't me condemning you. This isn't me judging you. I have no ability to do that. No, this is me warning you out of love, because I care about you! I care about your soul. I'm not attempting to use personal perception to scare anyone into following Jesus. Nor am I divulging my own opinions and views. How dangerous would that be when talking about such an important matter as your soul!? I'm only revealing what God has said in His Word. And I wouldn't be passionately cautioning you if it wasn't something Jesus did Himself. It is imperative that we look at Scripture and take from it what God has said about the matter. For me, this is where it finally became clear.

DON'T SHOOT THE MESSENGER

This brings us back full circle to where I led off in the opening chapter of this book. One night in college, I could no longer avoid this reality that was staring me directly in the face. I had run long enough, and I knew it. A few weeks prior to this night, I had begun reading the Gospels (Matthew, Mark, Luke, and John) with an attempt to study the life of Jesus. I concluded that I had avoided the Bible far too long, and would start trying to get into it more. It was the first time in my life I actually sat down and became intentional about reading the word of God on my own. I had one goal in mind: find out more about Jesus. I didn't want to be influenced by people, preachers, religious views, or culture. I wanted to learn for myself what that book had to say, and allow the Holy Spirit to instruct me every step of the way. I soon found myself fascinated with Jesus' teachings. At the same time I was convicted by the straightforwardness of his words and the boldness He spoke with. One of the most prevalent points of emphasis I noticed in His discussions and parables was eternity. I began to notice that he talked about hell just as much as he talked about heaven. I saw how He not only compared it to a prison of outer darkness (Matthew

8:12), but equated it to a place outside of Jerusalem (Gehenna, or the Valley of Hinnom) where pagan worshippers sacrificed their children to false gods by burning them alive. For those who think that fire won't be in hell, I advise you to merely glance at a few warnings Jesus delivers in the Bible. He makes it abundantly clear, making several fiery references throughout His teachings:

> *"They will throw them into the fiery furnace, where there will be weeping and gnashing of teeth."* (Matthew 13:42)

> *"If your hand causes you to sin, cut it off. It is better for you to enter life maimed than with two hands to go into hell, where the fire never goes out."* (Mark 9:43)

> *"Then he will say to those on his left, 'Depart from me, you who are cursed, into the eternal fire prepared for the devil and his angels.* (Matthew 25:41)

This is only some of what Jesus mentions about hell, not including other references that are given in both the Old and New Testament. One thing is apparent, Jesus did not shy away from talking about hell. But rather than reading those verses from surface level, I encourage you to go back later and deeply study them in context. I have found that anyone can twist Scripture to support and justify their claims. What I desire is for your eyes to be opened through prayer and studying for yourself, not simply by what someone else has told you.

One of the most vivid depictions that Jesus gives is in the story of the rich man and a guy named Lazarus. In Luke 16, we see this wealthy individual who lived a life of luxury. He dressed in puple and fine linen, and at his gate laid Lazarus. Lazarus was a beggar who desired to eat what fell from the rich man's table. From the passage, it is presented that the rich man ignores this beggar laying at his gate. Eventually, both men die. Lazarus is ushered to Abraham's bosom and the rich man is tormented in Hades. We see a heart-wrenching portrait of this fiery torment as the rich man pleads for help!

> *In hell, where he was in torment, he looked up and saw Abraham far away, with Lazarus by his side. So he called to him, 'Father Abraham, have pity on me and send Lazarus to dip the tip of his finger in water and cool my tongue, because I am in agony in this fire.'* (Luke 16:23-24)

As if this isn't enough, Abraham's response is even more shocking. He reminds the rich man that he had his good things during his lifetime, and Lazarus had bad things. But now the roles are reversed, informing him that he is receiving what is due to him. Even more troubling, he tells the rich man that it isn't possible for them to reach him and come to his aide. *"And besides all this, between us and you a great chasm has been fixed, so that those who want to go from here to you cannot, nor can anyone cross over from there to us.'"* *(Luke 16:26).* Not only does Abraham say that they can't reach the rich man, but that there is no possible way out for him; that no person can pass from there to where they are. The rich man makes one last plea – for them to warn his family so that they don't end up in the same place as him. Sadly, this request is also denied.

I remember one time reading this story and nearly weeping. I began thinking, "What if this is what it will really be like? What if we will see our friends and loved ones who didn't accept Christ being tormented, just as Abraham and Lazarus saw the rich man? What if we will hear them screaming at the top of their lungs in anguish? How much would it eat at us that it is too late to rescue them? I think it would it hurt us even more knowing that we had an opportunity to, by telling them about Jesus, and didn't!"

This alone should break us to have such compassion for those who aren't currently saved. Seeing eternity involves knowing what awaits those who don't accept Jesus, and doing everything possible to warn them. We can't force them to make a decision, and we certainly don't have the capability to save them ourselves. All we can do is plant the seed, proclaiming the Gospel and what it has done for us. Will the conversations be difficult at times? Yes. Will they be uncomfortable? Perhaps. Will you be concerned about how they view you? Sure. But our love for them should transcend any feelings of discomfort, and motivate us to tell them about the Good News of Jesus Christ. Unfortunately we worry more about offending them, than telling them the truth. But on judgment day, no one will be saying, "It's your fault for telling me the Gospel. You offended me to hell." Only, "You never told me!" We should be more concerned with what could happen to the soul of our unsaved friends if we don't tell them about Jesus, as opposed to what could happen to our friendship if we do.

I once refrained from sharing Christ with a friend, out of fear of what it would do to our relationship. When I finally built up the courage to have the conversation, it went way better than expected. He told me, "Kyle, you are the only friend I have who cares where I'll go when I leave here." What good is it to be together for a few short years on earth, but separated for eternity? That's not friendship. True love is telling people the truth, whether they want to hear it or not. Silence is the same as approval, and if we aren't telling others about Christ, we might as well be sending them to hell ourselves. People need the Gospel. There are millions who are unsure about this thing. And if that person is you, I'm telling you now that it is not too late. Jesus is the only way to heaven (John 14:6), and He's waiting for you to come to Him. If you already have, tell someone else!

BEHIND ENEMY LINES

The purpose here is not just to stress the reality of hell's existence. That is only one important element of the big picture. No, this is a reminder that we are to set our sight beyond the present. We are to remain attentive to that which surpasses our time here on Earth. As followers of Jesus, our entire focus should be on living in a way that personifies Him in every aspect of life. This is what seeing eternity is all about. This requires one thing – focus. It is easy to become preoccupied with life ventures that take our eyes off of Christ. No matter what we may profess, it is our actions that reveal what we are focused on. And for many, even those who may claim to be Christians, it is evident that eternity is not in their field of vision. In his epistle to the Philippians, Paul states that these type of people live as enemies:

> For, as I have often told you before and now say again even with tears, many live as enemies of the cross of Christ. Their destiny is destruction, their god is their stomach, and their glory is in their shame. Their mind is on earthly things. (Philippians 3:18-19)

Wow. I don't know about you, but I clearly hear Paul's crying heart in that passage. Read it again. His brokenness for others has led him to tears. Sobbing, he reminds the people of Philippi about the enemies of the cross of Christ – those self-indulgent people who might claim to be believers, but don't exhibit the life of sacrifice and selflessness that Jesus preached. I can't help but weep with Paul for those who are blinded by the pleasures of this world. I know so many Christians who are busy occupying their time with worthless and selfish deeds. Some of these very people are right inside the church. In turn, I often ask God to give me Paul's broken heart for those who are chasing after such vanity. Are you? Can we really say that we are weeping over their lost souls? Are tears streaming from our eyes in prayer as we intercede on their behalf, asking God to seize their hearts and save them? Being broken isn't just a realization of your own sinfulness. You begin to understand just how wicked and lost we all are as humans, and it equally breaks your heart. Not that you see yourself as perfect, but you see others around you who are lost and it tears you to pieces knowing that they are heading down a path of devastation. I've prayed constantly for friends I grew up with who are now living in sin. They are enamored by materialism, lovers of the night life, consumed with temporal values, and are slaves to pride. They are entangled in a life of habitual sin, and I can't afford to just sit back hoping that eventually they'll come out. They only see what is directly in front of them, focusing on the here and now. It is quite frightening. What's even more terrifying is their obliviousness to where it is taking them. Paul says their destiny is destruction. And if our love for these people is genuine, it should drive us to get on our faces before God pleading for their souls. I'm reminded of the words of Charles Spurgeon regarding this same matter. He said, "If sinners be damned, at least let them leap to Hell over our dead bodies. And if they perish, let them perish with our arms wrapped about their knees, imploring them to stay. If Hell must be filled, let it be filled in the teeth of our exertions, and let not one go unwarned and unprayed for."

In the same manner though, I believe this provides an opportunity to examine our own selves. The passage says, "Their mind is set on earthly things." It requires you to ask yourself: How much of my time and effort is spent on activities and interests that ultimately have no eternal worth? I once heard pastor and author, Francis Chan say, "Our greatest fear should not be of failure, but of succeeding at things in life that don't really matter." He was speaking in reference to eternity. While we may be constantly encouraged by society to attain wealth, pursue promising careers, and excel, in light of eternity these endeavors mean nothing. When you stand before God, He will not be concerned with your fruitless endeavors that did not advance the kingdom. He will not care about the amount of money you made during this lifetime, only what you did with it. He will not be impressed by your climb to the top of the corporate ladder, only who you told about Him on your way up. He will not reward you for the amount of times you clapped your hands and stomped your feet *in* church, but if you acted as the hands and feet *of* the church – living and serving as the body of Christ. God won't care about our achievement of the American dream, how many educational degrees and titles we obtained, or the number of commas in our bank accounts. What He desires is a life of obedience. He asks that you be an illumination of His glory everywhere you go. That your light shines so brightly amongst others, that (as the Scriptures say) they may see your good works, and glorify your Father in heaven." (Matthew 5:16). These works are not for self-glorification, self-satisfaction, or self-publicity. They point people directly to the One who has the power and ability to change their hearts.

Only what you do for Christ will count. And only what you do for Him will last! Paul even goes on to remind us that, as believers, we aren't to be concerned with temporary matters, for our residence is not in this world:

> *But our citizenship is in heaven. And we eagerly await a Savior from there, the Lord Jesus Christ,* (Philippians 3:20)

Seeing eternity means that we are to unceasingly live with eternity in view. All of our words, actions, and behaviors should be expressed with eternity deeply lodged in our minds. All of the activities we engage in and the endeavors we pursue should be with consciousness that we will appear at the Judgment seat of Christ. Revivalist Jonathan Edwards once said, "Lord, stamp eternity on my eyeballs!" Translation – "God, every word that I speak, every thought that I entertain, every decision I make while on this earth – may it be done with the understanding that one day I will stand before you to give an account for it! *"So then, each of us will give an account of himself to God (Romans 14:12).* As believers, we must be cognizant of this. Not that we are to spend this life tip-toeing on egg shells, but our endless love for God must be the driving force that moves us to walk the road of holiness each and every day.

But as for some, we see that they are enemies of the cross. I must ask you: Who do you know that is behind enemy lines? Who in your life has worldly tunnel vision that has spiritually blinded them to lose sight of what's most important? Even more important, what are you doing about it? If it isn't them, examine your own life. Regardless, it requires the same broken heart that Paul had, weeping with supplication.

"STARTING ROUTE TO.... ETERNITY"

I often use the Maps app on my phone when driving somewhere that I'm unfamiliar with. I type in the desired location and it provides me with a guided route to my destination. As I receive step-by-step instructions towards the end point, I'm generally careful to stay on the route that has been given to me. I turn when it says turn, and keep straight for the distance it tells me. But occasionally, I become distracted and accidentally make a wrong turn or bypass the exit that was commanded to be taken. All of a sudden, I find myself off course. Subsequently, I will hear the voice on my phone say, "Re-routing" as it attempts to provide an alternate route to get back on the right path.

Our turn-by-turn navigation in this life is the Holy Spirit. He empowers us to continue pressing on the right path, and convicts us when we begin to stray down the wrong one. The problem is that once many of us steer off course, we no longer seek to hear from Him. We turn off the navigation system, and delight ourselves in a joyride down Sin Street. We think it is better this way. There is no voice telling us, "Don't do it" and no warning signs telling us to turn around. Freedom! However, attempting to tune out the Holy Spirit so you can peacefully indulge in your sins doesn't remove their consequences.

We must come to realize that we have been given a choice; A choice to either continue along the path of selfishness and ruin, or to abandon that route, reprogram the GPS, and navigate ourselves to a destination of eternal life. I'm reminded of how Jesus talked about these very same paths to His disciples. He's conscious of them both and allows us to select which one we want to travel along. Yet, He is compassionate enough to provide guidance on which one He knows is best for us:

> *"Enter through the narrow gate. For wide is the gate and broad is the road that leads to destruction, and many enter through it. But small is the gate and narrow the road that leads to life, and only a few find it."* (Matthew 7:13-14)

Broken to Believe

The most frightening part of that scripture to me is Jesus' last few words regarding the road that leads to life: "…and only a few find it." At first glance, you would think that Jesus is talking about this road like it is hidden or something. When in reality, He's not referring to it as some secret pathway, but conveying that this road is not truly and wholeheartedly sought after by many. We would much rather be comfortable with walking the broad road and relying on grace, than seeking the narrow road to life.

This broad road that leads to destruction (hell) is heavily populated with traffic, and Satan and his team continually serve as the construction crew expanding it with more and more lanes. While Jesus is advising us to take the first exit ramp we see, many are opting to instead hit the cruise control button, turn up the music, put their turn signal on, and move into the fast lane. Sadly, once that destination of eternal destruction is reached, there is no opportunity to make a U-turn. Christian evangelist Leonard Ravenhill once said, "If there are a million roads into hell, there is NOT ONE out!" It is final.

Even after we decide to choose the right path, there are constant detours set up by the Enemy to sidetrack us. Satan's mission is to distract and deceive, luring as many people as possible away from Christ. He seeks to plant thoughts of doubt into your mind. He is constantly plotting schemes consisting of false philosophies and doctrine. He chomps at the bit to divert your attention from the light. And once he baits you away with curiosity, he will maximize any opportunity to attack and permanently destroy. Known as the god of this age, he has the ability to cause many to doubt:

"The god of this age has blinded the minds of unbelievers, so that they cannot see the light of the gospel of the glory of Christ, who is the image of God. (2 Corinthians 4:4)

This is why it is vital to stay near the cross. Constantly pray and ask God to keep your eyes on Him. Stay enveloped by the Word of God, and surround yourself with those who are going to encourage you to remain on the straight and narrow path. It certainly won't be easy. But we can't afford to test the waters of distraction, hoping a momentary experience won't pull us underneath. Stay focused. Your life depends on it.

NOW WHAT?

I pray this brings actual application to your life. I don't want you to walk away with temporary desires to "do better." Unfortunately, Christians do this on a weekly basis. We gather at church, hear a message, get stirred up for a while, and depart with no true change of the heart. We give it a mental thumbs up of approval, or an occasional, "That was a good message!" The emotional high might last throughout the day, maybe even a few days throughout week, but eventually the fire dwindles and there is a return to normalcy. At some point it has to become personal.

So what does this all mean? You might be asking yourself that. It means one thing: Believe. Believe with your whole heart that Jesus has called you. He has called you to believe in Him. He has called you to trust in Him. And most importantly, He has called to you live for Him! That is what this Christian life is all about. Personally, I don't want to get to the end of my life and realize I missed my whole purpose for being here. As Christians, it is absolutely possible for that to occur. I see it taking place all around us, and don't want that to happen to you. When it is all said and done, many will look back only to find that they missed the whole point! They went to church, sang the songs, prayed the prayers, and missed it this whole time! They were so concerned with this life, that they were eternally sightless. When we see God for who He really is, our whole outlook is revolutionized. He brings us to this broken state that seems to separate us from Him, but it actually draws us closer. The only way for this to happen is through intimate connection with God through prayer. Our brokenness must drive us to our knees in repentance. It puts into perspective our lack of obedience. And it shines a beaming light on our complacency. But it doesn't leave us there. No, we are broken for a reason. I believe God sees us in this state and smiles with joy. He is honored by our humility, and fills our broken hearts with never-ending gratitude! That is what moves us from broken to believing – the comprehension of His grace! That is what enables us to look past our current conditions, our meaningless pursuits, and our shortcomings – focusing our eyes and efforts on Him alone. Ask Him to give you the undying aspiration to serve Him with your whole life. God's unconditional love has brought you to this moment. What will you do? He wants you – All of you.

So we fix our eyes not on what is seen, but on what is unseen, since what is seen is temporary, but what is unseen is eternal (2 Corinthians 4:18)

Made in the USA
Charleston, SC
12 February 2017